In Jesus' Name

ISBN-13: 978-1-7326609-4-6

Contents

Preface

This book grows out of a conversation that took place in a home Bible study session. We were studying John's gospel, and one of my neighbors seemed somewhat agitated when we were discussing John 14:13: *"Whatever you ask in my name, this I will do, that the Father may be glorified in the Son"* (ESV). My neighbor felt that there must be something lost in the translation, because, as it is usually translated, it did not seem to be true. No one was satisfied with the discussion that followed.

My response was to read a number of readily available commentaries on the passage, and I was not completely satisfied with any of the interpretations of the passage that I read. I decided to meditate on the passage every day. That same week, in my daily Bible readings, I came to the passage in Matthew's gospel, where Jesus curses a fig tree.

> *"And seeing a fig tree by the wayside, he went to it and found nothing on it but only leaves. And he said to it, "May no fruit ever come from you again!" And the fig tree withered at once.* [Matthew 21:19 (ESV)]

I decided that the two passages were related, and I printed them out so that I could easily read them as part of my daily devotions. Eight months later, after reading these two passages day by day, I began work on this book.

Insights into these two passages have not come easily. I have started and re-started writing this book several times. Repeatedly, I have written a few pages, come to a stop, have set the book aside, and have worked

6

on something else. More than once, I have set this book aside for a month or more.

I have a passion for "getting it right" in God's eyes, and that God may be glorified. It's more than a desire to be faithful to God and to the scriptural texts. Much of the time I have not been at all sure that the book would ever be published.

Prior to writing this book, I published two poems that speak to the issues I'm sharing here.

WALKING IN FAITH
© 2001

Walking in faith is a challenge for fools and the brave. There are
Those who can see beyond sight, but we cannot trust those who seem
Fixed on their egos and lusts. That is what they become — they are
Self-centered czars of their followers' oft' shattered dreams.

Walking in faith with Our Lord Jesus Christ is for those who can
Let go of pride and find peace in submitting their will, and who
Seek to please only the One who redeems. There are those who can
Do this and walk not by sight, — but by faith and love too.

Walk not by sight but by faith we are told. We can hear and see
Miles of temptation to lure us to logic and safety. So
Much of our life is distorted by short sighted values. We

[continued]

Need to believe that there's Someone in charge here below.

Walking in faith is for those who are foolish enough to be

Trusting in God and in that which they cannot see. Then they find

That which is holy released in their humbleness, setting free

Power and clearing the ears and the eyes of the blind.

Walking in faith is the excellent choice for the people who

Suffer rejection and failure and loss. It is not for the

People who live perfect lives, for insensitive ones, those who

Think they're in charge. It's for those whom the cross has set free.

Prayer Is Like a Steering Wheel
© 1998

Prayer is like a steering wheel --
    it guides the roving mind.

It cannot be just sent-up flares to God
    for crises' sake.

To read of saints in scriptures feels
    like fuel so good to find.

We move through life and care to dare
    when evil's on the make.

So, prayer and power grow our faith
    as evil's left behind.

1.

What Did Jesus Mean?

According to John's gospel, Jesus made a promise that, on the surface, seems outrageous. After He had washed his disciples' feet, he had partaken of a final Passover meal with them, and Judas had left. He continued to talk with them, preparing them and comforting them with regard to what was about to take place. Then he makes this provocative statement:

> *Very truly I tell you, whoever believes in me will do the works I have been doing, and they will do even greater things than these, because I am going to the Father. And I will do whatever you ask in my name, so that the Father may be glorified in the Son. You may ask me for anything in my name, and I will do it.* [John 14:12-14 (NIV2011)]

There are at least two issues that must be addressed in this passage. When Jesus says that we can ask him for anything, the fact that He is fully divine as well as fully human means He sets no limits upon what we can ask. Hundreds of years earlier, God pointedly asked Jeremiah a provocative question that addresses this issue.

> *"Behold, I am the LORD, the God of all flesh. Is anything too hard for me?* [Jeremiah 32:27 (ESV)]

Accordingly, Jesus promises to do whatever is asked in order that the Father may be glorified. This motivation will be discussed later.

When the followers of Jesus pray, we often include the phrase "in Jesus' name." We hope – perhaps even know in our heart – God both hears our prayer and is granting our request. On Facebook, Franklin L. Smith pointed out that the phrase, "In Jesus' name" can be translated "under the authority of Jesus." He points to the Apostle Paul's letter to the Philippians:

> *In your relationships with one another, have the same mindset as Christ Jesus.*
> [Philippians 2:5 (NIV2011)]

Franklin Smith goes on to say, "If we are not praying according to His mind, we are not really praying in His Name."

Often our prayers are answered immediately, or eventually, in the affirmative. When time passes before we see an answer, many refer to "God's perfect timing." Jesus' promise in the above passage from John 14 does not seem to provide for such contingencies as the passage of time, however. If we take Jesus' promise at face value, He is telling us the answer will be yes when we ask in His name. This promise was expressed previously in another way after Jesus curses a fig tree shortly before His last supper:

> *Early in the morning, as Jesus was on his way back to the city, he was hungry. Seeing a fig tree by the road, he went up to it but found nothing on it except leaves. Then he said to it, "May you never bear fruit again!" Immediately the tree withered. When the disciples saw this, they were amazed. "How did the fig tree wither so quickly?" they asked. Jesus replied,* **"Truly I tell you, if you have faith and do not doubt, not only can you do what was done to the fig tree, but also you can say to this mountain, 'Go, throw yourself into the sea,' and it will be done. If you believe, you will receive whatever you ask for in prayer."**

(Boldface is mine.)
[Matthew 21:18-22 (NIV2011)]

There is a parallel to this passage that can be found in the 11th chapter of Mark's gospel.

History does not record anything even close to an instance where someone tells a mountain to cast itself into the sea, followed by the mountain doing so. While the followers of Jesus do not believe Jesus to be capable of lying to His followers or deceiving them, this passage naturally can lead some people to wonder: "What did Jesus mean?"

This is especially true for Christians like those who are in perpetual pain, asking Jesus for relief every day. When friends try to comfort or encourage them, to the person suffering their words can seem like useless platitudes even if appreciated. As an alternative, one can wonder if what Jesus said originally has been lost in translations through the centuries. Such an explanation offers no more comfort to the one suffering than any other.

When Jesus' closest friends heard him offer these promises, we have no evidence that His followers were surprised by what He said. In fact, we can be certain that they believed it. In the Book of Acts, there are several reports of miraculous healings that affirm that Jesus' followers believed what he had said and acted upon that belief.

The gospels and Acts affirm repeatedly that genuinely believing is essential to having prayers answered. Here are some examples.

In Matthew's gospel, the faith of blind men in Jesus led them to be healed:

> *As Jesus went on from there, two blind men followed him, calling out, "Have mercy on us, Son of David!" When he had gone indoors, the blind men came to him, and he asked them, "Do you believe that I am able to do this?" "Yes, Lord," they replied. Then he touched their eyes and said, "**According to your faith let it be done to you**"; and their sight was restored. Jesus warned them sternly, "See that no one knows about this."*
> [Matthew 9:27-30 (NIV2011)]

In Mark's gospel, a woman was healed in response to her faith in Jesus:

> *And a woman was there who had been subject to bleeding for twelve years. She had suffered a great deal under the care of many doctors and had spent all she had, yet instead of getting better she grew worse. When she heard about Jesus, she came up behind him in the crowd and touched his cloak, because she thought, "If I just touch his clothes, I will be healed." Immediately her bleeding stopped, and she felt in her body that she was freed from her suffering. At once Jesus realized that power had gone out from him. He turned around in the crowd and asked, "Who touched my clothes?" "You see the people crowding against you," his disciples answered, "and yet you can ask, 'Who touched me?'" But Jesus kept looking around to see who had done it. Then the woman, knowing what had happened to her, came and fell at his feet and, trembling with fear, told him the whole truth. He said to her, "**Daughter, your faith has healed you**. Go in peace and be freed from your suffering."* [Mark 5:25-34 (NIV2011)]

From the Book of Acts, Peter offers to heal in Jesus'
name:

> *One day Peter and John were going up to the temple
> at the time of prayer—at three in the afternoon. Now
> a man who was lame from birth was being carried to
> the temple gate called Beautiful, where he was put
> every day to beg from those going into the temple
> courts. When he saw Peter and John about to enter,
> he asked them for money. Peter looked straight at
> him, as did John. Then Peter said, "Look at us!"
> So, the man gave them his attention, expecting to get
> something from them. Then Peter said, "Silver or
> gold I do not have, but what I do have I give you. In
> the name of Jesus Christ of Nazareth, walk."
> Taking him by the right hand, he helped him up, and
> instantly the man's feet and ankles became strong.*
> [Acts 3:1-7 (NIV2011)]

Furthermore, from the Book of Acts, we're told that,
as the church grew, more and more people responded with
faith to what they heard was happening in the lives of
the apostles:

> *The apostles performed many signs and wonders
> among the people. And all the believers used to meet
> together in Solomon's Colonnade. No one else dared
> to join them, even though they were highly regarded
> by the people. Nevertheless, more and more men and
> women believed in the Lord and were added to their
> number. As a result, people brought the sick into the
> streets and laid them on beds and mats so that at least
> Peter's shadow might fall on some of them as he
> passed by. Crowds gathered also from the towns
> around Jerusalem, bringing their sick and those
> tormented by impure spirits, and all of them were*

14

healed.
[Acts 5:12-16 (NIV2011)]

These incidents make it clear that Jesus' disciples believed the promises He made. Perhaps it was easier for them to believe Jesus and have faith in his teachings because they heard him in person.

We know that Jesus understood this phenomenon because of what happened with Thomas after Jesus' resurrection. Thomas was not there in the upper room when Jesus appeared to ten of them on Easter, and Thomas was incredulous. A week later, Jesus appeared again. Thomas was there, and he expressed his belief. Jesus responded with compassionate understanding that it is easier to believe what you have seen.

> *A week later his disciples were in the house again, and Thomas was with them. Though the doors were locked, Jesus came and stood among them and said, "Peace be with you!" Then he said to Thomas, "Put your finger here; see my hands. Reach out your hand and put it into my side. Stop doubting and believe." Thomas said to him, "My Lord and my God!" Then Jesus told him, "Because you have seen me, you have believed; blessed are those who have not seen and yet have believed."*
[John 20:26-29 (NIV2011)]

Some may argue that Jesus provided this power to prayer only to those who knew Him and saw Him. After Jesus' apostles went on to heaven, however, miracles have since happened, even recently. Such is not frequently the case, however.

In November of 1997, a woman named Donna Pardue, suffering from the aftermath of a major stroke, saw her husband die. Shortly thereafter, her twin sister had a stroke, and her mother had a stroke as well. Donna asked the elders of her church in Shreveport, Louisiana to pray for her, that she could get some peace. Less than thirty minutes later, she was dancing and showing no effects of the stroke whatsoever. The next morning, after her doctor saw that Donna was no longer disabled, certified her as ready to go back to work.

In the summer of 2007, a young woman worshiping in Yosemite National Park was told that God was going to make Himself known to her in a tangible and powerful way. Driving back to college, she was in a head-on collision that destroyed her car and wrapped it around her. Using the "jaws of life," it took some major effort and time for her rescuers to extract her from the wreckage. At a nearby hospital, she was examined, but the woman suffered no broken bones or other major physical injuries. Still shaken up, she went home to stay with her parents for a few days.

The Apostle Paul, in his letter to the church in Rome, talked about the Holy Spirit's role in our prayers.

> *In the same way, the Spirit helps us in our weakness. We do not know what we ought to pray for, but the Spirit himself intercedes for us through wordless groans. And he who searches our hearts knows the mind of the Spirit, because the Spirit intercedes for God's people in accordance with the will of God.* [Romans 8:26-27 (NIV2011)]

Earlier in this chapter, Jesus was quoted from John's gospel regarding His doing whatever we ask in His name. He also says this:

> *"If you love me, keep my commands. And I will ask the Father, and he will give you another advocate to help you and be with you forever— the Spirit of*

truth. The world cannot accept him, because it neither sees him nor knows him. But you know him, for he lives with you and will be in you. [John 14:15-17 (NIV2011)]

Thus, when we ask in Jesus' name, we are involving the Holy Spirit. This brings us back to the initial question of this chapter. What does Jesus mean when he tells his followers to pray in his name, and He will do whatever we ask that His Father may be glorified?

Does asking in Jesus' name mean simply tagging the end of our prayers with the phrase "in Jesus' name?" If so, why are not more miracles taking place among Jesus' followers?

At the end of Mark's gospel, in the alternate second ending that is not in all the earliest manuscripts, Jesus tells his followers about some of the things that His followers will be able to accomplish after Jesus returns to heaven because of their believing through faith:

And these signs will accompany those who believe: In my name they will drive out demons; they will speak in new tongues; they will pick up snakes with their hands; and when they drink deadly poison, it will not hurt them at all; they will place their hands on sick people, and they will get well." [Mark 16:17-18 (NIV2011)]

Going back to John's gospel and the first quote, one thing of interest that cannot be ignored is Jesus' stated reason why His followers will be able to do such wondrous things:

*And I will do whatever you ask in my name, so **that the Father may be glorified in the Son.*** [John 14:13 (NIV2011)]

In response, a question we can ponder for ourselves is simply this: When we pray in Jesus' name, are we seeking to glorify God, or wanting God glorified in some way? Later, we will discuss the implications of this more fully. As we explore the implications of praying in Jesus' name, it leads us to ponder the relationship we have with God through Jesus.

Many psychological studies have concluded that successful relationships are built upon liking, loving, and trusting. With long-term relationships, there may be days when two people may not even like one another. Even during those days, however, a relationship won't falter if they love each other unconditionally and trust each other completely.

When something happens in our lives that we don't like, we may indeed blame God and not like what He has done. It helps when we know the Bible well enough that setbacks need to be seen in God's larger perspective. Some call it "seeing the big picture." Only rarely do the events of one day ruin the remainder of our lives. With determination and commitment, God can help us and redeem whatever happens as He glorifies Himself in us.

The Bible teaches us repeatedly that His plans are always bigger than ours. Once we gain that larger perspective, we can move on to what God has next prepared for us.

How much we trust God is a major factor in our relationship to God through Jesus. It is relatively easy to declare that we trust God, but our having a mindset in which we know we can trust God under all circumstances is something that typically takes time to develop. We may well reach a point of total surrender of our lives to God, trusting God with the process of life.

Of the liking, loving, and trusting that goes into a relationship, loving God can be a complex issue. We love God because God first loved us, which is true, and more.

> *"As the Father has loved me, so have I loved you. Now remain in my love. If you keep my commands, you will remain in my love, just as I have kept my Father's commands and remain in his love. I have told you this so that my joy may be in you and that your joy may be complete. My command is this: Love each other as I have loved you.*
> [John 15:9-12 (NIV2011)]

Here, we are challenged to remain in Jesus' love. What does Jesus mean when He tells us to remain 'in his love?' Since 1859, children have sung a hymn by Anna Bartlett Warner:

> *Jesus loves me! This I know,*
> *For the Bible tells me so;*
> *Little ones to Him belong,*
> *They are weak, but He is strong.*
> *Yes, Jesus loves me!*
> *Yes, Jesus loves me!*
> *Yes, Jesus loves me!*
> *The Bible tells me so.*

If remaining in Jesus' love involves belonging to Him, it is easy to take the next logical step and conclude that praying in Jesus' name may well involve our belonging to Him. We must not, however, jump to the hasty conclusion that praying in Jesus' name simply grows out of belonging to him and nothing else. Belonging to Jesus is a factor in praying in Jesus' name, but evidently it is not the only factor.

Once again, let's look at the issues raised with the phrase "in Jesus' name."

- ➤ Jesus tells us we'll get affirmative answers when our asking is in His name.

- ➤ Our relationship with God is reflected in how we ask.

- ➤ Our believing we will get an affirmative answer is essential to our asking.

- ➤ Our motive for asking is also essential.

- ➤ Our expectations of God affect the answers.

In the pages that follow, we will discuss these issues in detail. First, we will examine how Jesus teaches us to pray in more detail.

We will look at the "ingredients" Jesus includes in His "recipe" He gives His disciples when they ask Him to teach them to pray. According to Luke's gospel, Jesus gives them this example:

> *One day Jesus was praying in a certain place. When he finished, one of his disciples said to him, "Lord, teach us to pray, just as John taught his disciples." He said to them, "When you pray, say: 'Father, hallowed be your name, your kingdom come. Give us each day our daily bread. Forgive us our sins, for we also forgive everyone who sins against us. And lead us not into temptation.' [some manuscripts add] but rescue us from the evil one.'"* [Luke 11:1-4 (NIV2011)]

In Matthew's gospel, Jesus provides an example of prayer in His "Sermon on the Mount."

> *"This, then, is how you should pray: Our Father in heaven, hallowed be your name, your kingdom come, your will be done, on earth as it is in heaven. Give us today our daily bread. And forgive us our debts, as we also have forgiven our debtors. And lead us not*

into temptation, but deliver us from the evil one."
[Matthew 6:9-13 (NIV2011)]

As we consider what it means to pray in Jesus' name and/or with His authority, we need to consider how Jesus taught His disciples to pray in these two passages and in other. The Lord's prayer is not the only example we have of Jesus praying. Chapter 17 of John's gospel is almost entirely one extended prayer. We know that throughout His three years of public ministry, Jesus often withdrew to pray. By setting this example for His followers, Jesus teaches us the importance of prayer to our lives.

2.

Prayer's Ingredients

In this chapter, we are looking at the components that Jesus includes in His example we commonly call "The Lord's Prayer," which was quoted at the end of the last chapter from two of the gospels.

According to the original Greek language in which most of the New Testament is written, Jesus tells His disciples to address God as *Abba* or 'Father.' This is the form of address to God used by Jesus in the Garden of Gethsemane.

> *Going a little farther, he fell with his face to the ground and prayed, "My Father, if it is possible, may this cup be taken from me. Yet not as I will, but as you will."* [Matthew 26:39 (NIV2011)]

From this, we can conclude that Jesus wants His followers to address God as He does. This approach is more intimate or personal than simply 'God.' The Greek word *Abba* is a term of endearment indicating profound respect and love for a parent, although sometimes it is compared to the English words *Dad* or *Daddy*. We cannot assume Jesus' addressing God as *Abba* is somehow casual. The importance of our relationship with God will be discussed in more detail later.

In Jesus' model prayer, the next thing to say is "let your name be sanctified." It is important to express our awareness that God and His name are holy, and we want to treat God and His name as holy. Thus, in this model prayer, Jesus wants us to establish our humble attitude towards God, God's name, and God's holiness.

Having expressed our humble approach and attitude, we are to express our desire that God's kingdom may be just as obviously evident in His creation as it is in heaven. We also are to communicate our wish that God's plans and purposes be fulfilled within God's creation as it is in God's home.

Up to this point in Jesus' sample prayer, he has laid the groundwork for our requests to be made known for the occasion in which we are lifting up our prayers. Then, included with our requests, we ask that we not be tested, and that we be protected from evil. Finally, as demonstrated by Jesus' sample prayer, we are to surrender everything into God's almighty care.

With the rise of the Sunday Schools movement towards the end of the nineteenth century, a teaching tool was developed for use in Church School classes to help Christians remember these basic ingredients of prayer we have been discussing here. It involved an acronym with the letters **A-C-T-S-S.** These letters stand for:

A = Adoration and praise
C = Confession and contrition
T = Thanksgiving
S = Supplication (requests)
S = Submission or surrender

Although not everyone finds this tool useful, it is offered here as a summary of what Jesus teaches with his sample prayer. There is no indication that Jesus wants his followers to use all the ingredients of His recipe in all prayers. When Jesus cursed the fig tree, it was a straight-forward request and nothing else.

It is also not clear whether or not Jesus intended His model prayer to instruct His followers to follow His recipe in a particular order, but his sample prayer does follow a logical sequence. The longest prayer by Jesus in the Biblical record is in John's gospel, which takes up nearly all of chapter 17. That prayer does not follow the same format as the example he gave to his disciples to follow.

When praying in the name of Jesus or by His authority, we may use some or all the ingredients that we have discussed. Just as a cake is more than the ingredients in a recipe, it is also true that prayers are more than the words and phrases that are employed. Once again, let's keep in mind what the Apostle Paul told the church at Rome before he ever met them:

> *In the same way, the Spirit helps us in our weakness. We do not know what we ought to pray for, but the Spirit himself intercedes for us through wordless groans. And he who searches our hearts knows the mind of the Spirit, because the Spirit intercedes for God's people in accordance with the will of God.* [Romans 8:26-27 (NIV2011)]

The Holy Spirit is vital prayers and their answers. This will be discussed more later.

In my book, *Spiritually Growing Through Prayer* [©2018] I suggest a way of beginning an extended time of prayer that many people find challenging:

> As a person begins their time of prayer, they should ... try to focus upon God's presence, enjoying God's presence exclusive of all other thoughts. This sounds easy, but it can prove to be difficult, depending upon a person's personality. During this time, someone should not verbalize anything, aloud or silently.

Dr. Glenn C. Routt, a professor of theology at Texas Christian University for many years, called this ingredient of prayer "being present to God's presence." There are several things can happen when this is done.

> ➤ The clutter of everyday concerns may fall away.

> ➤ A sense of serenity may bloom inside the person praying because of resting in the Lord.

> ➤ While at peace, God may provide answers or responses to the concerns that prompted the time of prayer, without a verbalized question.

> ➤ During this quiet time God may also bring to our mind people or things that need to be discussed.

In today's world, this ingredient of prayer is especially challenging because it means letting the hectic pace of our lives come to a complete stop so that we can enjoy God. We can enjoy God's peace, mercy, grace, and love in an almost tangible way. In it, we find peace with God.

It can be logically argued that, if we do this for an entire day, we are resting in God and obeying one of the ten commandments:

> *"Remember the Sabbath day by keeping it holy. Six days you shall labor and do all your work, but the seventh day is a sabbath to the LORD your God. On it you shall not do any work, neither you, nor your son or daughter, nor your male or female servant, nor your animals, nor any foreigner residing in your towns. For in six days the LORD made the heavens*

and the earth, the sea, and all that is in them, but he rested on the seventh day. Therefore the LORD blessed the Sabbath day and made it holy." [Exodus 20:8-11 (NIV2011)]

When we engage in being present to God's presence, we are opening the door to having God's guidance during our time of prayer. We can readily see this in the Apostle Paul's comments to the Romans regarding the role of the Holy Spirit when we pray. As we practice engaging in this habit, we have an increasing sense of being humbler as we approach God with our prayers. In turn, our prayers become more in harmony with God's will and purposes.

In my previously mentioned book, *Spiritually Growing Through Prayer*, prayer is discussed more thoroughly than I will do so here, but I must emphasize two more things about one's overall prayer life. First, although Roman Catholics make confession and contrition a routine part of their prayer lives, other Christians frequently are not diligent in this regard.

King Solomon was emphatic about the importance of confession and contrition.

Whoever conceals their sins does not prosper, but the one who confesses and renounces them finds mercy. [Proverbs 28:13 (NIV2011)]

Since Christ died on the cross for our sins, many non-Catholics do not understand the importance of confession. Christ's youngest Apostle, John, does say this to Christians regarding their faith:

If we claim to be without sin, we deceive ourselves and the truth is not in us. If we confess our sins, he is faithful and just and will forgive us our sins and purify us from all unrighteousness. If we claim we have not sinned, we make him out to be a liar and

> *his word is not in us.*
> [1 John 1:8-10 (NIV2011)]

We know we are forgiven, so we can expose our sins in light of Christ's love for us. We can walk in faith with full knowledge that our slate is clean.

Acknowledging our dependence upon Jesus and His sacrifice for us helps us keep our perspective. The Apostle Paul expresses this in his letter to the church at Rome:

> *Therefore, there is now no condemnation for those who are in Christ Jesus, because through Christ Jesus the law of the Spirit who gives life has set you free from the law of sin and death.*
> [Romans 8:1-2 (NIV2011)]

M. Jack Suggs, a major authority on the synoptic gospels in his generation, told his students that approaching God in terms of Christ's Passion "has a way of clearing away the rubble between you and God." Thus, he encouraged his students to conclude that conversationally talking to God about our shortcomings and placing them at the foot of the cross is good for us spiritually.

Finally, we must never forget the importance of surrender. The phrase, "For yours is the Kingdom and the power and glory forever and ever. Amen." It may well be the oldest phrase of Christian writing after the New Testament. It can be likened to an abbreviated creed. This surrender phrase serves to put the rest of "The Lord's Prayer" and all of our prayers into perspective. When we surrender all that we are and all that we have to God, we are acknowledging our total dependence. There are no special words or phrases, and there are no special people with 'prayer power': Everyone is equal before God, who is always in command.

3.

Being in Christ

Thomas Chisholm was born in Franklin, Kentucky, in 1866 in a log cabin, and he and was brilliant enough to become a teacher as a teenager. He had a conversion and baptism in his twenties during a revival in Franklin. Shortly after the turn of the century, he became a Methodist Episcopal minister for a year before resigning due to health struggles. Limited in his mobility, Thomas Chisholm turned to writing as a vehicle to live out his faith.

In those struggles, he wrote many Christian poems and hymns over the remainder of his days. In 1917, he wrote *Living for Jesus*, which was set to music, one of the most memorable songs of his 93-year life. It is the third verse that introduces this chapter.

> Living for Jesus wherever I am,
> doing each duty in his holy name,
> seeking the lost ones he died to redeem,
> bringing the weary to find rest in him.

If, according to Chisholm, living for Jesus includes "doing each duty in His holy name," could he mean that praying in Jesus' name means praying out of a life lived in Him?

In Luke's gospel, Jesus relates part of His own fulfillment as *Messiah* to his followers.

> *Then Jesus asked them, "When I sent you without purse, bag or sandals, did you lack anything?" "Nothing," they answered. He said to them, "But now if you have a purse, take it, and also a bag; and*

> *if you don't have a sword, sell your cloak and buy*
> *one. It is written: 'And he was numbered with the*
> *transgressors'; and I tell you that this must be*
> *fulfilled in me. Yes, what is written about me is*
> *reaching its fulfillment."*
> [Luke 22:35-37 (NIV2011)]

In response to what Jesus says here, we may logically ask, how are His disciples part of His fulfillment? In this chapter, we will explore the answers to these questions.

At least part of the answers is provided by Jesus, when He talks about His disciples breaking bread with one another and with Him.

> *Whoever eats my flesh and drinks my blood has*
> *eternal life, and I will raise them up at the last day.*
> *For my flesh is real food and my blood is real drink.*
> *Whoever eats my flesh and drinks my blood*
> ***remains in me***, *and I in them.* [boldface mine]
> [John 6:54-56 (NIV2011)]

When we eat and drink, that food becomes part of ourselves. When we eat and drink Him, as we remember His last supper, He becomes part of us and of our lives. It is an intimate act that is repeated within communities of faith as a part of worship. It reminds us that we are in Him as He is in us.

Jesus confirms this during His last week before His death, burial and resurrection.

> *Before long, the world will not see me anymore, but*
> *you will see me. Because I live, you also will live.*
> *On that day you will realize that I am in my Father,*
> *and **you are in me**, and I am in you.* [boldface
> mine] [John 14:19-20 (NIV2011)]

Here, once more Jesus talks about His being in us and, interestingly, our being in Him. Here, we are getting a fuller understanding of what it means to be "in Christ."

Later, Jesus goes into greater detail.

> *Remain in me, as I also remain in you. No branch can bear fruit by itself; it must remain in the vine. Neither can you bear fruit unless you remain in me. I am the vine; you are the branches. If you remain in me and I in you, you will bear much fruit; apart from me you can do nothing. If you do not remain in me, you are like a branch that is thrown away and withers; such branches are picked up, thrown into the fire and burned. If you remain in me and my words remain in you, ask whatever you wish, and it will be done for you.*
> [John 15:4-7 (NIV2011)]

Here, in verse 7, we are given the same promise that we have at the beginning of this book in John 14. Without equivocation, Jesus tells us simply to ask.

Now we can shift our focus to see this issue from the Apostle Paul's point of view. He states very clearly what it means to have Christ be in us, and for us to be in Christ.

> *Therefore, there is now no condemnation for those who are in Christ Jesus, because through Christ Jesus the law of the Spirit who gives life has set you free from the law of sin and death.*
> [Romans 8:1-2 (NIV2011)]

While in this passage Paul speaks of our being in Christ as being not condemned, he states this reality in an even more positive way in his correspondence with the church in Corinth.

> *So, from now on we regard no one from a worldly*
> *point of view. Though we once regarded Christ in*
> *this way, we do so no longer. Therefore, if anyone is*
> *in Christ, the new creation has come: The old has*
> *gone, the new is here!* [2 Corinthians 5:16-17
> (NIV2011)]

Since we are a new creation when we are in Christ, our
humanity is, in a sense, enhanced by Christ's presence
within us.

At the beginning of the chapter, two questions were
raised:

> ➤ Could it be that praying in Jesus' name means
> praying out of a life lived in Him?

> ➤ How are His disciples part of His fulfillment?

Answering the second question first, it appears that
being in Christ and living for Him makes us part of His
ongoing work of spreading the good news and doing the
things that He did. In this sense, praying in Jesus' name
means we can be born of His power and authority. The
Apostle Paul confirms this in his letter to the Colossians.

> *For in Christ all the fullness of the Deity lives in*
> *bodily form, and in Christ you have been brought to*
> *fullness. He is the head over every power and*
> *authority.* [Colossians 2:9-10 (NIV2011)]

With all that Jesus tells us, and which is enlarged
upon by the Apostle Paul, it is clear that Christians need
to pursue the greater effectiveness of prayer that Jesus
offers us.

Eli Stanley Jones (1884–1973) was a 20th-century
missionary and theologian. Remembered chiefly for his
interreligious lectures to classes in India, he helped to re-
establish Indian forest retreats as a method of bringing

people together for days at a time to study their own spiritual nature. He said,

> *Out of the quietness with God, power is generated that turns the spiritual machinery of the world. When you pray, you begin to feel the sense of being sent, that the divine compulsion is upon you.*

In chapter 2, we discussed the importance of being present to God's presence. E. Stanley Jones obviously understood this, and that God's power is closely connected to God's presence.

With a different perspective, William Clement Stone was a businessman, a philanthropist and an author of self-help books. He was born in 1902, and his father died three years later, leaving his family in debt. Beginning in 1908, he peddled newspapers while his mother worked as a dressmaker. By 1915, he had saved enough money to buy his own newsstand for $100. Over the remainder of his life, he turned that $100 into millions with a desire to succeed coupled with brilliant business sense, becoming a true rags-to-riches man. As a philanthropist, he also became an 'angel' to others, lifting some out of poverty to great wealth and success. He often said the Bible was "the world's greatest self-help book." He also said, "Prayer is man's greatest power!"

Edward Perronet (1726-1792) believed prayer's power is specifically in Jesus' name. In 1780, he published eight verses in his most famous hymn, "All Hail the Power of Jesus' Name." It is commonly associated with two different tunes, and frequently referred to as "The National Anthem of Christendom." Most Protestant churches today are familiar with less than half of the verses. The first verse, published anonymously in 1779, illustrates our point here:

All hail the power of Jesus' name! Let angels prostrate fall; bring forth the royal diadem, and crown him Lord of all.

As it was pointed out in the first chapter, the followers of Jesus often close their prayers with the phrase *in Jesus' name*. Whether or not the person praying recognizes the significance of the phrase '*in Jesus' name*' is open to question.

> ➤ Jesus tells us we'll get affirmative answers when asking is in His name.

> ➤ Our relationship with God is reflected in how we ask.

> ➤ Our believing we will get an affirmative answer is essential to our asking.

> ➤ Our motive for asking is also essential.

> ➤ Our expectations of God affect the answers.

Our Expectations

All too many followers of Jesus do not consider how our expectations of God affect the answers. Such expectations can only be based upon the nature and character of God.

Most people can readily understand that God is omnipotent – all powerful. As it was pointed out previously, there is nothing too difficult for God, and God says so in the Bible, in Jeremiah 32:27. "*I am the LORD, the God of all mankind. Is anything too hard for me?*" (NIV 2011)

In a similar way, most people can understand God is omniscient – that there is nothing that God does not know. The youngest apostle of Jesus says this: "*If our hearts condemn us, we know that God is greater than our hearts, and he knows everything.* [1 John 3:20 (NIV 2011)]

Understanding God is all-powerful and all-knowing goes a long way towards understanding the attributes of God, but the one quality of God that is often misunderstood is that fact that God is eternal. The word 'eternal' does not refer to an infinite length of time. Albert Einstein is sometimes quoted as saying, "God created time so that everything won't happen all at once." Since God created time, God is present apart from time.

This leads us to a final and important attribute of God: God is *omnipresent*. This means that God is present in every place and every time because God is eternal. No one can fully comprehend all of these attributes of God, so even the very idea of God is humbling.

In a very real sense, our expectations of God could be infinite. This is why it is important to study the Bible, which reflects God's character. Everyone's expectations of God grow out of their understanding of what the Bible reveals concerning God, along with their prayers and meditations over what they read there.

Our Motives

Our motives for making requests of God are also essential. Jesus says, "I will do whatever you ask in my name, so that the Father may be glorified in the Son." John 14:13 (NIV2011) When we intercede on behalf of someone, most of us want our prayer to be answered for that person's benefit. When we pray on behalf of ourselves, most of us want to benefit from the answer God provides. This is understandable, but Jesus seems to be asking more of His disciples. Can we not hope that God will be glorified in the answer to our prayer? It is not that all of us are selfish, but that Jesus wants us to look beyond ourselves.

Our Believing

By position, we're not talking about physical position, such as standing, kneeling, or lying down. Some people prefer to pray with their eyes closed, while others keep their eyes open. Prayers said aloud can help us focus our thoughts, but silent prayers are also highly respected.

By perspective, we are not talking about the relationship with a person for whom we are praying. It also has nothing to do with the vantage point of a situation. We are coming back to a point made earlier.

The Apostle Paul told the Romans to be constant in prayer (Romans 12:12). He told the church in Thessalonica to pray without ceasing (1 Thessalonians 5:17). He also told the Colossians to continue steadfastly in prayer (Colossians 4:2). Although Jesus told parables about being persistent in prayer, that is not the issue here.

Our Relationship

Our relationship with God is reflected in how we ask. Consider how Jesus spoke to his disciples on the day prior to his arrest and trial.

> *No longer do I call you servants, for the servant does not know what his master is doing; but I have called you friends, for all that I have heard from my Father I have made known to you. You did not choose me, but I chose you and appointed you that you should go and bear fruit and that your fruit should abide, so that whatever you ask the Father in my name, he may give it to you.* [John 15:15-16 (ESV)]

Notice how Jesus says we are his friends, and that He chose us so that we would bear fruit. Earlier in the chapter of John's gospel, Jesus says we are to *remain* or *abide* in Him, and He describes Himself as the *true vine* from which we are to draw his strength and power, bearing His fruit. We are to be His friends who are an extension of Himself. If we are asking out of our relationship with His vine, the fruit we bear glorifies His Father.

> *"Truly, truly, I say to you, whoever believes in me will also do the works that I do; and greater works than these will he do, because I am going to the Father. Whatever you ask in my name, this I will do, that the Father may be glorified in the Son. If you ask me anything in my name, I will do it.*
> [John 14:12-14 (ESV)]

Asking in His Name

Jesus tells us we'll get affirmative answers when asking is in His name, while abiding in His vine.

> *"I am the true vine, and my Father is the vinedresser. Every branch in me that does not bear fruit he takes away, and every branch that does bear fruit he prunes, that it may bear more fruit. Already you are clean because of the word that I have spoken to you. Abide in me, and I in you. As the branch cannot bear fruit by itself, unless it abides in the vine, neither can you, unless you abide in me. I am the vine; you are the branches. Whoever abides in me and I in him, he it is that bears much fruit, for apart from me you can do nothing. If anyone does not abide in me he is thrown away like a branch and withers; and the branches are gathered, thrown into the fire, and burned. If you abide in me, and my words abide in you, ask whatever you wish, and it will be done for you. By this my Father is*

glorified, that you bear much fruit and so prove to be
my disciples. [John 15:1-8 (ESV)]

The Greek word μένω, transliterated menó, almost
always used to be translated in the New Testament as abide,
which isn't a word used often any more. Recent translations
of the Bible translate menó as remain to make the language
current. It is true that "remaining" is a critical part of the
meaning of menó. However, translating menó simply as
"remain" is, at best, a compromise.

Less obviously than simply remaining, menó in the
Greek language implies continuing on as things are, clinging
to hope, clinging to life. Menó means continuing unchanged
against adversity.

For example, Jesus asks His friends to be present with
Him in the garden of Gethsemane, where Jesus says to
Peter, James, and John, "My soul is very sorrowful, even to
death; remain [menó] here, and watch with me."
[Matthew 26:38 (ESV)] While it is true that they remained
in the place where Jesus left them, they failed to do as Jesus
asked. Why?

It is true that menó entails physically staying in place.
It also entails continuing to live, "to keep on keeping on."
Menó can in addition mean unchanging, continuing to be
strong, and having a common purpose. In the garden, Jesus
seems to want Peter, James, and John to endure the coming
storm, to not let their minds be distracted, but to wait with
Him. He wanted them to be with Him emotionally and
spiritually as He prayed to His Father in heaven. They did
not manage to do so, and they left Him alone. They did not
abide [menó] with Him.

As quoted previously, Jesus says,

> Abide [menó] in me, and I in you. As the branch cannot bear fruit by itself, unless it abides [menó] in the vine, neither can you, unless you abide [menó] in me. I am the vine; you are the branches. Whoever abides [menó] in me and I in him, he it is that bears much fruit, for apart from me you can do nothing. If anyone does not abide [menó] in me he is thrown away like a branch and withers; and the branches are gathered, thrown into the fire, and burned. If you abide [menó] in me, and my words abide [menó] in you, ask whatever you wish, and it will be done for you. By this my Father is glorified, that you bear much fruit and so prove to be my disciples.
> [John 15:4-8 (ESV)]

In other words, if we live and menó [abide] in Christ, we will bear His fruit, endure, wait unchanged, and be one with Him, showing His love. Now, we can see an even larger picture. The answers to our prayers asked in Jesus' name are the fruit that comes from abiding [menó] in Him as we pray.

4.

In Christ's Presence

In the second chapter, one of the "ingredients" of prayer was labeled with Glenn C. Routt's phrase, "being present to God's presence." It is important that we return now to discuss this further.

When a person first hears this phrase, it is natural to think of public worship services. In Protestant services, the worship leader often begins with an invocation: It is a prayer that asks for God to be present to bless the worshipers as they worship together. Although we know that God is present everywhere at any time, the prayer nonetheless "invokes" God's presence. Ideally, the people worshiping have an acute awareness of God's presence as they worship.

One can also think of being present to God's presence in private or solitary worship. In such cases, a person can engage in solitary prayer in a number of ways. Countless people have talked with God while walking in a wilderness. The same can be said of praying aloud while driving a vehicle down a road. With a little effort, a person can seek out a place of solitude in which to talk with God. When engaging in these prayer activities, a person often has a sense of intimacy in these prayer conversations, particularly if a person is reading or hearing scriptures, or if they are listening to music written for Christians.

There is another intimate approach to God's presence that may or may not include solitude. When discussing our expectations of God in the third chapter, we examined how our understanding of who God is can powerfully affect our prayer life. Since no one can take pictures of God or scientifically analyze God's existence, we can only analyze our relationship with God. We do so in terms of the Bible's descriptions of Him. Here's a review:

> - God is omnipotent – all powerful, with no limits. God created all the universe.
> - God is eternal – lives outside of time and its constraints. God created time.
> - God is omniscient – knows everything in creation because of existing apart from it.
> - God is omnipresent – is present everywhere at every time.

It is this fourth attribute of God that needs to be considered in our efforts to be present to God's presence. Since God is present everywhere at every time, we can practice being aware of God's presence in any situation. Some simple examples can illustrate this point.

When worshiping in church, it is relatively simple to imagine God hearing what we sing, what we pray, and what we hear. We can imagine God's receiving our efforts to worship Him. Doing this, the sincerity of our worship seems enhanced.

When silently traveling, whether down a highway or in some other context, it is also easy to imagine Jesus being with us, seeing what we see and hearing what we hear. Going further, we can imagine Jesus seeing what we see, hearing what we hear, and experiencing what we are experiencing during any activities of our lives. With practice, this type of experience is both habit forming and rewarding to our overall spiritual life.

Once we get into the habit of being present to God's presence in our worship and our travels, it becomes easier to be present to God's presence in all situations as we live out our lives throughout the day. As we do so, we approach accomplishing the Apostle Paul's admonition to pray without ceasing.

> *Rejoice always, pray without ceasing, give thanks in all circumstances; for this is the will of God in Christ Jesus for you.* [1 Thessalonians 5:16-18 (ESV)]

Once we establish being present to Christ's presence as we live and move throughout our days, we can easily recognize this as what Jesus means by abiding or remaining in Him. According to Christ, this is how we bear His fruit.

Jesus does this as they are walking across the Kidron Valley on their way to the Garden of Gethsemane. Although the valley begins north of the city and extends to the Dead Sea, this part of the valley is east of the Temple. It was his commonly taken route between Jerusalem and Bethany, where he often stayed with friends.

The Vine and Its Fruit

As they are walking from the upper room to the Garden of Gethsemane, Jesus describes His Father in Heaven as the *vine* dresser, or as the *vine cleaner*. This was familiar material for His disciples. Vine dressing or vine cleaning is normally done during the Spring. If it is done earlier in the year, the vine might be damaged by late frost. In John 15, Jesus describes Himself as the "true" vine. In the Old Testament, the people of Israel are often referred to as a grape vine. In contrast, a wild vine does not yield the kind of juice that makes good wine.

Jesus tells His disciples, *"Already you are clean because of the word that I have spoken to you."* [John 15:3 (ESV)] As disciples of Jesus who pay attention to what He teaches, we are *clean*. When a grape vine is cleaned, most of the previous year's growth is cut and removed. Metaphorically, this means that our pasts are merely history, and we are growing fresh in Him. Any vintner will testify that grape plants are robust and forgiving. If a person cleaning a vine makes a mistake and removes too much, it probably doesn't matter. Our vine cleaner, God, does not make mistakes, however.

This metaphor from Jesus is richer and deeper than most people realize. After a vine is cleaned in the Spring, the remaining canes (branches) begin to produce fresh shoots, which produce leaves and fruit. Fourteen to sixteen leaves well-exposed to the sun produce the richest and most abundant fruit. If there are too many shoots, there cannot be enough leaves exposed to the sun, and that reduces the size of the crop. The vine cleaner begins thinning the shoots in the early summer so that the vine can bear more fruit. In terms of our metaphor, if we spend an excessive amount of time studying and discussing our faith, we will not yield as much fruit from the vine.

We, the branches, bear fruit for others to consume. We bear fruit to feed others spiritually – to make other disciples, to feed the faith of other disciples, and to grow and multiply the faith of others.

In another sense, our presence in the lives of others can provide Christ's nourishing and healing presence. When Jesus dwells in our hearts as our Savior, best friend, and constant companion, Jesus is there to be at work in us. This is what it means when we say that the church is the body of Christ.

Thanksgiving and praise are the lubricants of all relationships, both human and divine. Praising and thanking God in both public and private worship are essential to our relationship with the Divine. Old Testament worshipers brought in the first fruits as sacrifices to God. Beginning in the New Testament and continuing into the present, worshipers bring the "fruit" of our lips to God, glorifying God with our praise. We bring all that we are, surrendering ourselves to the Father, the Son, and to the Holy Spirit. God can then glorify Himself in us. Our world produces temporary happiness and entertainment. True love and devotion come from our abiding or remaining in Christ. We can sleep for a night, but true rest and peace come from God, with Jesus dwelling in our hearts.

Being branches of the vine, we represent Christ and sow the seeds of the gospel. Winning souls is a process. The Apostle Paul put it this way to the people of Corinth:

> *I planted, Apollos watered, but God gave the growth. So neither he who plants nor he who waters is anything, but only God who gives the growth.*
> [1 Corinthians 3:6-7 (ESV)]

Even if we plant or water the seeds of the gospel, we may or may not witness the harvest. Meanwhile, we are representatives of Christ and part of His church, which is His earthly body. Those of us who abide in Christ and share our lives with others are encouraging one another towards the holiness of Christ.

Leading others to Christ is only a beginning. Communities of faith then have to help new believers learn the teachings of Jesus, how to follow Him, and how to pursue being like Him. Teaching new Christians to abide in Christ by being present to God's presence in prayer is a very valuable lesson to learn. Leading others to Christ means sharing what is ours through Christ. This is the best stewardship of who we are in Christ. We invest ourselves in Him. This then can lead the believer into being the hands, eyes, and ears of Jesus in the community. Furthermore, Jesus might lead someone into another community, where He uses us there.

5.
Praying in Jesus' Name

Previously, the third verse of "Living for Jesus" by Thomas Chisholm was quoted. This final chapter begins with looking at the first verse.

> Living for Jesus, a life that is true,
> Striving to please Him in all that I do;
> Yielding allegiance, glad-hearted and free,
> This is the pathway of blessing for me.
> Refrain:
> O Jesus, Lord and Savior,
>   I give myself to Thee,
> For Thou, in Thy atonement,
>   didst give Thyself for me;
> I own no other Master,
>   my heart shall be Thy throne;
> My life I give,
>   henceforth to live,
>   O Christ, for Thee alone.

This hymn could easily be seen as describing someone who is abiding or remaining in Jesus. If we are striving to please Him in all that we do, then our prayers are going to reflect that effort:

1. Our adoration and praise will reflect our desire to please Him.
2. Our confessions of our shortcomings and sins will reflect our genuine desire for Jesus' blood to wash away our sin and our striving towards His holiness.

3. Our expressions of thanksgiving for deliverance from evil and receipt of other blessings will reflect our relationship with Jesus.
4. Our prayer requests will reflect our hope to see God glorified in our prayer's answers.
5. Our surrender to Him will be that of all we have and all we are.

Our resulting life of prayer will reflect our understanding that we are praying in Jesus' name, even if we don't say that we are doing so. We will be praying in the power of Jesus' name, and we can pray with the power and authority of Jesus' name.

Now we can understand Jesus' seemingly outrageous promise in the fourteenth chapter of John's gospel.

> *Very truly I tell you, whoever believes in me will do the works I have been doing, and they will do even greater things than these, because I am going to the Father. And I will do whatever you ask in my name, so that the Father may be glorified in the Son. You may ask me for anything in my name, and I will do it.* [John 14:12-14 (NIV2011)]

There are, in fact, no limits to what we can ask for in prayer. After all, nothing is too difficult for God, and Jesus wants the Creator of the Universe to be glorified in the answers to our prayers. As we have seen, the timing of God's answers to our prayers is perfect, so it is not really a concern for us.

When we are living in and for Jesus, everything in this life is merely a prelude to eternal life. While hanging on the cross, Jesus spoke to one of the thieves who was crucified next to Him.

> *One of the criminals who were hanged railed at him, saying, "Are you not the Christ? Save yourself and us!" But the other rebuked him, saying, "Do you not*

fear God, since you are under the same sentence of condemnation? And we indeed justly, for we are receiving the due reward of our deeds; but this man has done nothing wrong." And he said, "Jesus, remember me when you come into your kingdom." And he said to him, "Truly, I say to you, today you will be with me in Paradise."
[Luke 23:39-43 (ESV)]

After the prelude of this life, we leave behind diet plans, pain, bifocals, canes, medications, walkers, and wheelchairs. God's timing is relevant only in this life, not the next.

Jesus' followers enjoy seeing God glorified in the answers to our prayers. We often do not notice, however, when God glorifies Himself in our lives. Albert Einstein is famous for saying, "Coincidence is God's way of remaining anonymous." Those who keep a prayer journal, however, can often see answers to their prayers in 20/20 hindsight.

The Acts of Jesus' apostles illustrate how literally they believed Jesus' promises. A number of miracles are associated with Jesus' followers. In today's world, we seldom hear about miraculous answers to prayers. In part, the truth of this is illustrated by something said by French author Ludovic Halevy in 1834:

"No news is good news."

Following this logic, truly good news is not news, so it is seldom published. Magazine publications such as *Christianity Today* and *Charisma* often cite apparent miracles, but these occasions are the exception. The fact remains that miracles still do happen, and Christians enjoy opportunities to recognize God being glorified, and we offer our praises in response.

It is important to remember that truly believing is essential to seeing our prayers answered. We see this emphasized in Matthew 9:27-30, in Mark 5:25-34 and elsewhere. This was discussed previously. We also discussed how Peter illustrated the importance of belief in Acts 3:1-7. It is obvious Jesus' disciples had faith in His teachings and believed His promises.

In today's world, all of us can learn from Thomas' experience. At first, Thomas did not believe that Jesus was resurrected from the dead, but when he met Jesus and saw the Lord's wounds believed. Jesus' observation in response offers us a critical lesson as we conclude this book.

> *Jesus said to him, "Have you believed because you have seen me? Blessed are those who have not seen and yet have believed."* [John 20:29 (ESV)]

Thomas did not believe the miracle of the resurrection until he saw Jesus. Then and now, God glorifies Himself in miraculous events. The followers of Jesus seldom see Him today, but we believe in the resurrection, and that He is alive. Naturally, we are reluctant to believe a miracle has occurred unless we witness it with our own eyes. Believing by faith is as much of a challenge now as it was then.

God's spirit plays a vital role in our prayers, as the Apostle points out in Romans 8:26-27, which we have discussed. Those of us who love Jesus understand provides the Spirit to help us (John 14:15-17). When we ask for something in the power and authority of Jesus' name, we are involving God's spirit. It is important to believe it.

We learn from the gospels that when we are asking with belief, we are not to ask selfishly, but with the hope that the answer glorifies God. This brings us back to the idea that we're more likely to witness glorious answers to our prayers when our requests grow out of our relationship with God, out of our abiding in Jesus and having Him in our heart. As with any intimate human relationship, that rapport of hope involves liking loving, and trusting. Trusting God is the key to our hope. Back in 1996 I wrote a limerick about this.

> Living in fear we can't cope.
> Living unhappy we mope.
> Trusting in God
> Is the path that we trod
> Because hope that is seen is not hope.
>
> Living in joy we can cope —
> Faith conquers our steepest slope!
> Trusting in God
> Is the path that we trod,
> For we're living in joy, faith and hope.

God's plans are invariably larger than ours. When we try to see things from God's greater perspective, it is much easier to keep moving towards tomorrow. It is quite easy to declare our trust in God, but to do so unconditionally can at times require great effort on our part. Surrendering everything to God only gets easier with practice.

Jesus tells us to abide (remain) in His love. It is one thing to sing about Jesus' love for us, however, living it out and loving Jesus in return is a challenge worth pursuing. It involves belonging to Him. Jesus tells us we will get positive answers to our prayers when asking in His name. Jesus wants our requests to reflect our relationship with Him.

When Jesus is in our hearts as our Savior, best friend, and constant companion, and when we're constantly trying to abide in Him, the resulting relationship must be of absolute trust. We must trust in Him and in His promises. We must also want what Jesus wants – that God is glorified in the answers to our prayers. This vital relationship with

God through Jesus leads us to expect great things because God is God.

Jesus led a prayer-centered life here on Earth, so much so that His disciples asked Him to teach them to pray. Christ's teachings and examples provide us with encouragement to pray in His name – in the power and authority of His name. Our decision to follow Him shapes us in this life and into eternity.

Other Books by James J. Stewart
Available at Amazon

Christian Inspiration, Study, and Poetry

Faith and Yosemite:
Fourth Edition
[Christian poetry with
pictures of Yosemite]

Faith Fuel
[Meditations on the
Christian faith and life]

Lasting Love
[Short Biographical Sketches]

Living for Jesus
[A Gospels Study Guide for
Couples and Small Groups]

Deliberately
Growing Spiritually
[A five-year Bible reading
program for spiritual
transformation.]

Seed Thoughts for
Christian Prayer
and Meditation
[Workbook]

Single Sentence
Sermons
[Workbook for growing faith]

Walking in Faith
[Much of the same poetry as
Faith and Yosemite but
without pictures]

Spiritually Growing
Through Prayer
The focus is upon personal piety
and spiritual growth through
prayer.

Christian Fiction

The Camera Doctors
[Two people meet on top a
famous mountain, and
romance ensues.]

Casting Lots
[Christian romance and
adventure set in the near
future]

Christian Romances
in the Foothills
An anthology of Tom's Town,
Soul Mates, &
The Camera Doctors

An Extensive Life
[The life story of a man who
lived more than
four hundred years.]

Empty Tomb,
Full Hearts
[A Selection of Testimonies
Among Those Who Saw
the Risen Christ]

The Gaardian Saga
[Christian science fiction
fantasy with God in a major
role.]

52

A Nation Transformed
*[A future tale of God
intervening in the USA with
miracles.*

A Second Call to Serve
*[A tenth-generation pastor and his
second wife accept a call to build a
church from scratch.]*

Prayer Warriors
*[Urban adventures in a near-
future continuation of
Casting Lots]*

Soul Mates
*[Romance, the same setting as
Tom's Town]*

This World Is
Not My Home
*[Two together since high
school separate to find love
with others.]*

Tom's Town
*[Small town life and
Christian romance]*

The Warrior and the
Prophet
*[God has surprises and
blessings for newlyweds]*

Yosemite Picture Books

Ever-Changing Yosemite Valley
*[Yosemite Valley is a glacially carved valley. Moment by
moment, scenes change.]*

Faith and Yosemite Fourth Edition
*[Pictures of Yosemite National Park,
with poems about the Christian faith]*

Portraits of El Capitan
*[El Capitan rises 3000 feet above the floor of
Yosemite Valley]*

Portraits of Half Dome
[Half Dome marks the east end of Yosemite Valley]

A Sense of Wonder: Yosemite
*[A Christian poem about Yosemite,
illustrated with pictures]*

Starlight Over Yosemite
[Large pictures of Yosemite taken at night]

Yosemite Textures and Shadows
*[High definition photographs of Yosemite Valley,
depicting all seasons, both day and night.]*

"Hallelujah I am Woman"

"Hallelujah I am Woman"

A woman's worth God's precious

"Hallelujah I am Woman"

"Hallelujah I am Woman"

ISBN 978-0-6151-6435-9

All scriptures are from the King James Version.

Published in the United States of America

A Woman worth God's precious gift 4

Introduction

This guide is a motivational tool that will inspire women of all nationalities and lifestyles. I pray that God blesses you as you read these inspiring pages about healing, self renewal, strength and your worth as a woman. In this life, we as women have suffered many disappointments, which in turn have caused an episode of industrious women to evolve all around the world. We are growing in vast numbers in many industries; we are showing our talents and strengths like never before. It is my honor to bring you more edifying words as you all seek your goals. I pray that all your journeys be successful, with many blessings.

"I now send you to open their eyes, in order to turn them

from darkness to light." (Acts 26:17-18)

There is times when we need someone to illuminate what we already know in our hearts. However, it is always encouraging to hear words of motivation.

"Hallelujah I am Woman"

At the tender age of 5 years old, a family member molested a young girl. Then again, at the most confusing time in a young girl's life at the age of 14, this same young girl raped by someone she trusted a school counselor.

Ridiculed by everyone; hate had set up its home in a bright, intelligent young woman who had big dreams of becoming a Doctor and a Writer. Within a moments Notice, her dreams, crushed with nightmares, pain, loneliness and despair. For many years she lived with the pain of not being able to live above

Shame, a UN forgiving spirit grew heavy in her heart, especially, for her mother:

"Because a mother is supposed to protect you" at least That is what she thought. Although, she could not forgive her Mother, she still knew in her heart that her mother had great love for her. As the years passed, she lost even more hope, living the life of a teenage mother; never really knowing what a child hood was. As if the pain was not enough, she married an abuser of women, alcohol, and drugs, which took her pain to another level. Divorcing the

first husband, and believing that she had met someone better, she married

husband number two; different names, same man, the cycle continued. You see that young girl was me Betty Knight-Taylor. However, that is the old woman. The new woman can shout, "Hallelujah, I am woman!"

On a rainy Sunday Morning in November, God showed up and showed out in my life, releasing me from the pain, of generational curses. Today, my Mother and I have a great relationship. Ladies, you are not defeated. The devil

"Hallelujah I am Woman"

is a liar, I call on Jesus to bind him and throw him, and all his friends back in the pit of hell where they belong. You see, he, (the Devil) looked into my future. Saw God had planned great things and the devil thought he would kill me before I received it. The Devil did not get the victory on that one, I am still here (Praise God) and I will get back everything the devil stole from me, why? Because, God said so!

"Hallelujah, I am woman," this phrase is more than just words. "Hallelujah!" This comes from deep with in my soul. Being woman is something admired, many of us *cannot identify with our worth as women due to lack, shame, and self-doubt. I truly honor being a gift from God, a virtuous woman in every sense of the word I have discovered who I am in God, for many years, I did not know. I had no idea of the value I hold as a woman. Now, that I know who I am, I want to share this message God has given to me to share with his women through ministering in written word. This message is not to tear down but, to build and uplift your spirits right where you are. I want this message to be a Blessing to all women.*

You may have experienced some of the things in this message or know someone who is going through the perils of these discussions. I pray for your strength. I pray that God opens your ears and your eyes that you may see his many miracles evolve in your life.

God's plans for Women are beginning to bring renewal of spirits and knowledge to women everywhere. Our strength lies in our ability to unite and become one mind under the guidance of the Holy Spirit.

Key Statement: Your strength lies in your faith and prayers.

Proverbs (16:9) "A man plans his way, but the lord directs

his steps.

God will lead you to your destiny if you acknowledge Him in your dealings; He will help bring success to you. When we seek God's will, we can rest assured that everything will be better than all right. Trust God, he has his way of doing things, Ladies; I want you to have the best God has for your spiritual, physical and emotional growth I pray that as you read this book that you will build a relationship or renew the one you have with our Lord and Savior Jesus Christ; he is waiting to refresh you. Reach out, take his hand, and let him lead you to a victorious life. In the beginning, God created man and

woman. According to the bible, God created Man first. Genesis (1:26) In addition, God created Woman as well.

Genesis (2:18) Woman was taking from man's rib and given as a gift to man.

Woman was created to be man's helpmate, friend and confidante. God gave man instructions as to how to love the woman. This is one of the reasons women should shout, "Hallelujah I am woman" with strength, boldness and all honor to God.

However, many of us are afflicted with issues of low self-esteem. The issues surrounding women continue to rise at alarming rates. Women we should be cherished in our households; nonetheless, many of us are afraid to go home.

Do you realize we are the true essence of life given by God almighty? Look at the name God and Adam gave us.

WOMAN, Think about it, when you look in the mirror

this is what you should see.

W = WISDOM, far more precious than rubies and diamonds.

O = OUTSTANDING, you should stand out as a virtuous woman.

M = MIRACLES, we bring forth life.

A= ANNOINTED, by the blood of Jesus.

N= NURTURING to the mind, body, and spirit.

This should be a celebration yet, we are hurting in so many ways from many adversities. We suffer from low self-esteem, anger, bitterness, unfaithfulness, and hopelessness A lot of us cannot comprehend our worth because; it was not portrayed in our households as young girls coming up and in most cases today it still is not being taught, or led by example. We must begin to break these Generational curses that have plagued our very being in society today as a whole.

"Hallelujah I am Woman"

Do you understand God gave us as a gift to man?

That is a real love offering God bestowed on man. Woman has the ability to be everything to man and earth. We are the strength that helps to hold the family structure together. How can you not celebrate that? I am thankful to God that he has given me insight as to who I am as a woman; however, there was a time when I did not celebrate this awesome standing of purpose, I simply did not know my worth. Becoming a woman of virtue is a process; age has nothing to do with becoming a Woman. The first step in becoming a woman and most of all, a "Godly woman," is to know who you are.

God has given all of us women a purpose in life. We are here to carry out assignments. We are to utilize our time here on earth; we must go about doing the things of the lord and not sit idly letting our purpose pass us by. We are the fruit of the earth, which is to bear witness to the goodness of the Lord.

Key Statement: learn what your purpose is and connect to success through prayer and supplication.

"Hallelujah I am Woman"

Genesis (1:26) "And God said let us make man in our image, after our own likeness. God is awesome! He made Man after his own image, so, when we look at one another we see the image of God. Genesis (2:18) "And the lord Said, it is not good for man to be alone; I will make a help meet for him." This is how "Woman" came to be.

"Hallelujah I am Woman"

Notes

WHAT SEEDS ARE YOU SOWING?

What are you sowing as a woman? Everything you plant is coming up. Sow your seed in good soil, so your prayers will not be hindered. What you sow, you shall also reap. What have you been sowing that would cause shame and lack in your life? I sit doubt, anger, discontent, or a non-forgiving spirit? If so, these unsettled spirits can wreck havoc in your life, causing you to Miss God's blessings. These attitudes are negative and can derail you from the true happiness that God has intended for you. We all have suffered negative situations in our lives.

These negative spirits can be a hindrance, if allowed to become a part of our lives. Circumstances can make us or break us. Which will you allow to happen in your life? I know that negative things such as divorce, abuse, and poverty can drain us of our energy. Of course, this is not God's plan. However, we have a choice. We have free will to make decisions concerning our lives. No, we do not always make the right choices. However, we can learn from *our mistakes to bring blessings into our future. I know I have made some bad choices concerning some of the issues I have had to face nevertheless, this is not an excuse to give up we should strive for excellence. Whatever, you have a passion for in life should drive you to your purpose so that you can see your goals become realities.*

Key Statement: Be conscious of the choices you make when you are striving for excellence.

HAVE FAITH AS YOU PURSUE YOUR GOALS.

All hope and blessings come from faith. Without faith, it is impossible to please God. (Hebrews 11:1) "Now faith is being sure of what we hope for and certain of what we do not see." We must have faith that what we are pursuing will happen as we speak the will of God for our purpose in life. The bible says,

"Faith without works is dead." Can you imagine living a dead life? You should want to be all that you can be in your time here on earth. (James 2: 14) What good is it, my brothers, if a man claims to have faith but has no deeds? Can such faith save him? Notice, if you are not pursuing God's will with actions of love and Forgiveness in your hearts.

Without faith you are not able to experience the grace of God. You have God's grace to be in his presence. Everything you do, you are doing it in God's presence. Let your works edify your faith. We all have a measure of faith given to us by God. Unfortunately, your self-esteem can be shattered to the point that you feel worthless. That is a lie from the pit of hell.

You are unique and original with your own God-Given talent no matter who you are, or where you come from; you can succeed with your gifts. We are multitalented individuals. You have to know what your talents are and bring life to them. Have faith that your creator has started a work in you that he will bring to finish by faith; your prayers will honor God as you please him with your faith to pursue your goals this will bring miracles in your life as the will of God is edified through your faith. You have the same ability to accomplish your goals as well as the next person. You must stay focused on a daily basis. Being successful and fulfilling your goals will take work, nevertheless, you have to set your priorities. When we set our priorities, we can better focus on our goals. Sometimes there will be things that will come against you, but you cannot let it stop you from what you have set out to do. Keep your faith in tact; stay prayerful about what you are doing. We as women can be very resourceful when we set our minds in the right directions. Women take on mighty challenges as you put your faith in Jesus.

We are taking our families to higher dimensions, as we take on the duties of being the head of our households. God is anointing Women with strength like never before. Our time has come to reap the harvest in Jesus name.

"Hallelujah I am Woman"

Notes

"Hallelujah I am Woman"

ARE YOU A SINGLE WOMAN, OR

SINGLE MOTHER?

I know for a lot of you sisters out there being single can be hard at times. I was a single parent. However, this is not all bad. I was married for a number of years to a man I loved very much. After many years, I found myself alone and sick to my stomach. It can be heart breaking after so many years of being in a relationship to find yourself alone facing responsibilities that God left for the head. (Man)

"Hallelujah I am Woman"

At first, my days would consist of crying, not eating and just plain feeling worthless. I felt as if I was a loser because my marriage was in ruins. It ultimately ended in divorce; it is a life changing experience to say the least to have shared so many intimate details with a man who betrays you. You go through the same stages of grief as you would if that person has passed on. The pain is even greater when another woman is involved. I know most of you, if not the vast majority, know exactly what I am talking about.

"Hallelujah I am Woman"

Now listen, you have a choice to make at this point, you could lay down for the count or you can get up and show the world what you are made of.

It is ok to have a pity party, but you must move on. Life cannot get better if you do not initiate a plan to make it better.

You are in full control with God by your side. One thing about God, he is always there to help you overcome any situation. All you have to do is acknowledge the fact that God is your source.

Nevertheless, in order to bring Joy into your life you have to first, understand there is a healing process you must go through to achieve your goals of success as you gain strength through prayer and confessions. Being single is a time that you can start living your God-given purpose as a woman.

Let your light shine so that everyone can see your confidence. When you portray confidence people notice it. You cannot help anyone until you help yourself. Your children are depending on you for their support, lean on Jesus as you go through your day.

Raising children as a single parent can be very challenging. We as mothers have to portray an image to our sons and daughters. We must teach our children the ways of the lord, in order to train them to Know right from wrong. Although, there is times that no matter what we do our children will stray. This is the time we must stay prayerful.

Have faith that God is going To take care of any situation you may find yourself in as a parent and especially, a single parent. (Proverbs 22:6)

"Train a child in the way he should go and when he is old he will not turn from it."

You can rest assured that your teaching and hard work will not be in vain. I know it seems as if the days will never end, especially when you have to do it all by yourself. Hold on, keep your faith my sister, help is on the way. It is a new day. You are a new woman. Get up and start your day by acknowledging your maker. What is done is done; keep your faith and prayers strong that you do not fall under attack. Start seeking your goals in life, live your purpose; it is not too late to enjoy life. Shake those life-threatening stresses out of your mind and body.

Do you know who you are? If not, let me tell you. You are the daughter of the high king. You deserve to be treated with greatness. Do not wait on anyone's permission: get up, get out and live!

Key Statement: Being single and a single mother does not mean you are hopeless, live your life with grace.

Enjoy your life as a single woman, not only can you grow closer to God, this will also give you time needed for your physical and Spiritual healing. Spend this time to raise your children in a healthy atmosphere. Sometimes, you need to stay single for your growth, many of us women rush to be in a relationship only to find that what you rushed into is not what you really want.

Take the time to know God, draw close to Jesus and let him choose your mate.

"Hallelujah I am Woman"

We go out looking for someone without consulting God and end up with misery and discontent, so to avoid a broken heart and spirit trust God he knows just what you need.

God is only going to give you his best in everything concerning you, but you must be able to receive when God is blessing you. The man that God has for you may not come in the package you anticipated, it's easy to miss your blessings by judging the outer appearance.

A lot of you miss it because you are not taking the time to see the real man.

The Man that God has for you, may not come wealthy, college educated or that Knight and shining armor that you dreamed about as a little girl. He may very well be just the opposite of all that dreamy stuff. I know one thing for sure, when God sends him your way and he is a God fearing man then he is everything you need in a husband.

"Hallelujah I am Woman"

Notes

LOVE THE WOMAN IN YOU

You are woman, Original and unique. There is no other like you. There are women all over the world that have no love for themselves. Sure, if you ask most women if they love themselves the answer is going to be yes, 9 out of 10 times. However, it is not true. In most cases, the negative aspects of abuse, divorce, alcohol and drugs have shattered the self-love that women should have.

These spiritual demons have robbed us women in many ways that it has become an epidemic; many beautiful lives have been shattered from these tragic incidents.

The devil came to steal, kill and destroy not only the human race but also us women because we are the bearers of life. We can easily fall prey to these tragic episodes if we do not stay prayerful. You must watch everything around you so that you do not become a statistic to the harmful environments. When you love the woman in you things will go smoother. Women who love themselves will not allow unrighteous happenings. So many times, we *want to love and be loved we want the affection of a loving man in our lives.*

However, you cannot gain love if you do not have love or respect for yourself.

The bible says that "the power of life and death rest in your tongue."

Speak life into your Circumstances, start speaking the opposite of your present status. Claim it by faith.

(Proverbs 18:21) "The tongue has the power of life and death and those who love it will eat its fruit."

Believe it and receive it in Jesus name. We call our lives into existence by the things we say. If you are speaking negative things, guess what, you will receive just that: the negative. Always speak positive with love especially to yourself. Sometimes we have to encourage ourselves for that motivation to keepgoing after our goals. **(Proverbs15:4)"The tongue that brings healing is a tree of life but a deceitful tongue crushes the spirit."**

Believe in yourself; believe that you have the strength to do all things through Christ who strengthens you. Speak healing words into your spirit so you can bring life to your whole body. God has called you to a purpose. Keep yourself in a manner that is pleasing to God. Anything you do will ultimately have an outcome. Love yourself and watch how things will start to come to life as you continue your journey towards your goals, success is going to happen.

(Proverbs 16:3) "Commit to the lord in whatever you do and your plan will succeed."

We must portray morals and integrity that our children can see this being lived in our lives so they will have something to go by. You must have that self-love in order to produce love. When we love who we are our children see health in our lives, this gives them the confidence needed to see life in a healthy way. Love will abound in your household as you speak the will of God. Love, speak love, and live love, this is a spirit that can conquer negative spirits; you can turn your circumstances around by giving love and receiving love.

Do this daily so your life will edify you as the loving mother, wife, friend and child of God.

RELEASE NEGATIVE LOVE.

Married or single, letting go of negative love can be one of the best decisions you will make. There is no positive in negative love. You are in love with someone that cannot return the love you shower him or her with is not deserving of your energy or time. When you allow yourself to be subject to neglect, you are setting yourself up for major disappointment.

When a man is in love with you, he wants the best for you. Many women are in love all by themselves; this has to stop with you. Ladies have some dignity about you. Do not tolerate someone treating you, as if you are not important. God gave you as a gift to operate, not to live a life of emotional abuse and pain. Your worth is far more than rubies and diamonds. **(Proverbs 31:10)** you have the right to be treated as the gift you are. It saddens me to see so many women stay in abusive relationships where they are controlled by fear. How can he say he loves you, if he is beating you? Not only are you hurting yourself, but *the children, if you have children you are hurting them as well. Usually, they grow up thinking this is normal when in reality it is not.*

You are charged by God to protect your children from the tragedies of the world.

Why would you subject yourself to this type of life? Most times this is from poor images of you. If you have to fight in your home to get the man you Love to see your worth you are fighting a losing battle. The only way he is going to change is if he is ready to make the changes necessary to be the man that God has called him to be. I have talked to many women who stay in loveless relationships

because they think they are not capable of making it alone or they make excuses to be with someone who mistreats them on a regular basis. We were not created to be treated with disrespect. We are women that are precious in God's eyes. You have to make a choice and some changes in your life. In this type of relationship, you are allowing yourself to be a woman that is not valued, when you accompany yourself with people who do not respect your position. A negative relationship, without the necessary changes will always bring discontent in your spirit. What will it take to see this man does not love you? Your name is not the one related to a female dog, black eyes, broken body parts and being publicly humiliated. **(Proverbs 14:17) "A quick tempered man does foolish things and a crafty man is hated."**

Any man who suffers you to violence do not understand righteousness, his spirit only knows destruction. Sister, you are the daughter of the highest King who loves you more than anyone does. God has a purpose and a plan for your life. The devil is a liar. God has great things for you!

Therefore, what your man told you, he's all you need and you will never amount to anything or have anything that is truly a curse.

The enemy wants to keep you in bondage, and at his total command. Listen, a man that abuses you in any way has no love or respect for you. Matter of fact, he has no love for himself, There is nothing that you can do to change him, he has to want to change. If he loves you then, change will come. Pray for God to deal with him.

My sister you need to pray and ask God to make a way for you to get out of bondage. Do not stay in a relationship like this hoping that things will get better, they are more likely to get worse, and you need to leave when your life is in danger. Give that burden to God. Let go and let God fight your battle.

(Matthew 11:28) "Come to me all who Are weary and burdened and I will give you rest."

God wants you to have a life without pain and worry. Please be wise on how you handle a relationship like this. When it is time for you to leave, pack your bags and go! Pray and ask God to lead and guide you. Women have died from staying in abusive relationships. I lost a sister and a friend behind this. Please, seek God and find a place where you can go where you and your children will be safe. Be careful about your move.

Remember, it is not good to tell people everything, especially when you are leaving an abuser. Your girl could be the one to give you up. Lord, I pray the prayer of protection over the lives of any woman going through an abusive relationship. You know the pain she is going through. Jesus, please make a way for her to Leave;

I pray that your will is done in their lives.

Peace, harmony and a renewal of spirit will rest in abundance. Thank you in advance Father God because I know that you are able to restore my Sister in Jesus name, amen. Stop holding onto the things that keep you feeling anxious, afraid, down, depressed, and stressed. Search deep in your spirit and ask Jesus to show you a better way of living so That you can gain confidence needed to carry out your mission to get to your goals. It is ok to think about those past issues, hurts and pains that will sometimes surface.

However, do not dwell there; use it to remind you this is not how you want your life to be. It is ok to remember, this will cause you to gain the strength needed to move on to greater things that God has for you.

(Proverbs 20:19) "A gossip betrays confidence: so avoid a man who talks too much."(In this case a woman.)

It is time to release him, it, them, or whatever else that is hindering your growth.

God is ready to pour out his blessings and a fresh anointing into your spirit.

However, you have to release whatever it is that is hindering you from getting to the place where God has called you to be. God wants us free! We cannot move to the next level unless we let go and let God.

Key Statement: Move to the next level by allowing God to remove you from hindering spirits.

When you are holding onto to negative hurting circumstances you are holding God from taking the situation. Give it to him and let God do the work for you. Your problem is never too big for your heavenly father.

"Hallelujah I am Woman"

Notes

Notes

YOUR SELF ESTEEM

Self-esteem is our birthright; it is ok to toot your own horn. This is a self-fulfilling act of appreciation for who you are. When you like who you are, you are able to share your appreciation with others. Be sincere with yourself and true to who you are as a woman, do not hide your true feelings. If someone does not know who you are, they usually cannot give you the love you deserve. Always try to surround yourself with positive people. Pamper yourself psychologically, spiritually, and emotionally so that you are able to experience a positive mindset.

Instead of tearing down your self-esteem, learn to build it. Celebrate your accomplishments; your self-esteem is influenced by many factors, self-esteem comes from how we have been nurtured in our lives as young girls to Women.

Choose to hear positive life sustaining words. This will bring self-confidence as you pursue your goals, which will allow your journeys to be happier. No one has the right to belittle you; no one has a right to say they are better than you are. The only way someone can kill your self-esteem is if you allow him or her to crush your spirit with negative, envious speech.

The majority of us were raised in homes where our own family members speak lack, and negative spirits into our lives. They hurt our feelings and lower our perception of ourselves.

Now as women some of us are still accepting this bad behavior, It is time to set the record straight and stand bold and announce that you are a child of God and you will not allow anyone to kill your self-esteem anymore now, praise God, hold your head high, and walk away with your victory. Never let anyone make you feel less than the woman you are. Remember you are a gift from God and that says it all. When you start to study God's word it will bring healing to your spirit. Start to meditate on the things of God and let the Holy Spirit guide you as you walk in Faith, you will begin to speak healing, walk in righteousness as you continue to seek the Kingdom of God everything about your spirit will come alive, your self-esteem will begin to rise to greater levels.

I had to pray for God to strengthen me, my self-esteem was in the gutter, I never saw myself as pretty, smart or worthy of anything good. My *experiences in childhood were so devastating I thought of suicide many times. I thank God for the grace he laid in my life, the mercy and love he shadowed me with his loving protection. As I started my journey of faith and becoming the woman God has caused me to be has changed me into a totally different person. I no longer see my life as a disaster, but as a blessing that I can share with others who are in pain. God turned my life around that I am now a blessing to others, which is an accomplishment in itself. I can now say that my life is great!*

LEAVE THE MARRIED MAN ALONE.

Sisters, if you never hear another word I say please, listen to me now. A married man is not the man you want to have a relationship with. For many reasons but, the main reason would be to keep your relationship with God in a righteous state.

A married man that cheats on his wife should be a red flag to any woman. That man's wife is a woman just like you; she has feelings, which can be damaged, from your disrespect of her position. Marriage is a holy union. When you get in the midst of the union, you are committing an act against God, Yourself, the wife and the man you are sleeping with.

You have taken your worth as a woman to an all time low. How would you feel if someone was sleeping with your husband behind your back? The thought of that feels bad. Well, how do you think his wife feels? No one is worth going to hell over especially, a married man. Get your own man! Pray that God sends your husband. The man he has for you. When God gives his man, you will get his best. A man that will love *you and God is the best man to have. First, you are repositioning yourself to seconds; no doubt, his wife is first. He is not going to leave his wife and children for you.*

Why would you want a man that would abandon his wife and children?

Look at it this way, when he goes home he goes to his wife, when holidays come around you got it he is with his family; he spends his money at home paying bills for his family. This man pass away whom do you think gets his inheritance? Well certainly not you, that is right, the wife. Now, tell me again what makes you want him. Sorry my sister this is not a good enough reason for God to allow you his blessings. If you want God's blessings then you need to leave Mr.Married man alone. See, you do not want to jeopardize your relationship with your father in heaven over a romp. **(Proverbs 6:12) "But a man that commits adultery lacks judgment; whoever does so destroy himself."**

Remember, what goes around comes around; this is also (reaping what you sow) you do not want to sow or reap the fruit of adultery, Stay Prayerful and classy as you are, Mr. Right will come in God's time.

Key Statement: Never seek love from another woman's husband.

You do not want to hinder your prayers with the spirit of adultery. When you are sleeping with another woman's husband, you are in risk of judgment from God. Not only do you weaken your spiritual health but also, your physical health is in danger. If he is cheating with you, he may very well be cheating with other women as well. This can leave you vulnerable to many social diseases. Remember, honor marriage and have respect for yourself. **(Proverbs 5:15-17) "Drink water from your own cistern, running waters from your**

own well (16) "Should your springs overflow in the streets your streams of water in public squares? (17) "Let them be yours alone never to be shared with strangers.

God wants you to have your own husband and a man to have his own wife. We must teach our daughters about the dangers of sleeping with married men, not only should we teach our daughters we should show them by example, by being a Virtuous woman with standards and morals that they may see our faithfulness to God. When they see that marriage is honored in your life, it will give them a sound understanding of how to handle this situation.

Not only will you have a better relationship with God, you will also have a better relationship with yourself and your children as well. A woman that uses sound judgment is a woman of virtue, she is defined as a woman of wisdom that cannot be mislead by temptation of lust. As I write this book I am a single woman, I desire for God to send my husband to me, I am patiently waiting for my earthly king to come into my life, the one that will bring that abundance of love and respect for me.

When we allow God to take control of our destiny we cannot go wrong. God sincerely wants us to be happy, not living a life of stress in relationships with married men, which will only bring heartache.

BE A VIRTUOUS WOMAN IN YOUR MARRIAGE

Wives do not give up on your marriage. Being married is not an easy road to travel. However, it is well worth the walk.

Hebrews (13:4) "Marriage is honorable in all, and the marriage bed undefiled. Nevertheless, whoremongers and adulterers God will judge.

The enemy wants to destroy your marriage, finances, peace, health, and ultimately your children; marriage is a gift from God.

The bible says,

"When a man finds a wife he has found a good thing."

This is another confirmation to your worth as a woman.

(Proverbs 18:22) "He who finds a wife finds what is good and receives favor from the lord."

When problems occur in your marriage, it is always wise to take it to God in prayer.

(Matthew 19:6) "So they are no longer two but one therefore, what God has joined together let no man separate."

"Hallelujah I am Woman"

This means that no one is to interfere in your marital vows and you in turn are not to let anyone have that power. God's purpose is for man and woman to dwell together in harmony and be monogamous in the marriage. This is also with the blessings of children within the union. Anything other than this type of relationship is sin. Sinful relationships Include; Fornication, (pre-marital Sex), homosexuality and adultery. Our father in heaven will judge these type relationships. Stay prayerful daily for your marriage. Not everyone can give you advice about your marriage so, it is important that you are seeking God first to lead you. The power of God comes from your sincere prayers, take authority over the issues concerning you and your mate. Keep praying and believing with forgiveness in your heart.

However, the bible says that every wife should be submissive to her husband. I have found that in order for you to be submissive to your husband, in turn he must be a man worth submitting to. **(Ephesians 5:22)"Wives submit to your husbands as to the lord (23) for the husband is the head of the wife as Christ is the head of the church. (25) "Husbands, love your wife just as Christ loved the**

church and gave himself up for her."

With a loving heart you should fulfill your duties as a wife, as you would do it unto Christ, your husband should not be disrespected.

(Proverbs 12:4) "A wife of noble character is her husband's crown but a disrespectful wife is like decay in his bones." *If this happens, you are setting yourself up for problems to arise in your marriage.*

"Hallelujah I am Woman"

(Proverbs 14:1) *"The wise woman builds her house, but with her own hands the foolish one tear hers down."*

The sad part is that it can be something as simple as not cooking for your husband. Men are attention seekers and when they do not get the attention they desire, they have the tendency to act out, so it is very important that you always keep your man satisfied and I do mean your righteous man, the one that is taking care of his business as a man of God and as a husband to you.

When a man is righteous in his dealings with God, he is going to be a man that you will happily submit. A righteous man has the understanding of your worth as a woman; he knows that you are his precious gift that God has bestowed to him.

Key Statement: A good wife always respects and loves her husband. A good husband in turn will cherish his wife.

(Proverbs 31:11-12) "Her husband has full confidence in her and lacks nothing of value. (12) "She brings him good, not harm, all the days of her life.

A good wife will help her husband to grow. When a woman is righteous, her husband can depend on her in his *time of need. Your husband should never have to look to someone else to carry out the duties you have promised to do before God and man.*

Do not let others tell you how to handle your relationship he is your husband. Treat him as the man God blessed you with.

Stop finding fault in your Husband and help him to come to a better understanding as you speak the will of God into his life as his helpmate.

The little things can cause so much misery, when the communication dies, then, there is a good chance that your marriage will. Be a virtuous wife; back your men up in their decisions, if what he does fail, do not beat him up for it. Talk it over without making him feel less than a man. Pray and love your man he will come around.

When you are always treating your man as though he is your child, he will eventually start to resent you. Your husband is your earthly king, when he is being the man that God has called him to be then your position as a wife is generally easy.

"Hallelujah I am Woman"

I have seen women mistreat good men, leaving them bruised for the next woman. When a man has been hurt he is more reluctant to commit because of fear. We must be careful in how we treat the men in our lives, now if he is a man that is not deserving of your love then that's different. My advice to you is to seek a way to end this relationship, because it will only take you to places that will diminish you as a woman. However, you have to be in a position that warrants your decision.

Circumstances such as Adultery and abuse are warranted reasons; no one wants to live a life of depression. That kind of life is not living, you are just existing. Remember, God wants you to experience a fulfilled life with abundance in every area.

STOP IMITATING OTHERS

We live in a copycat society. One person does something most people have the tendency to follow suit with the same thing. Be yourself. Originality is an asset whether you know this or not. Being yourself speaks your worth as a woman.

"I do not want to be anyone but, Betty."

Trying to be someone else only shows your lack for originality. Think for yourself, have your own ideas and creative ways of doing things.

Your success will play a big part in how creative you are. Your plans will have to consist of what you want and how to do it.

(Ephesians 5:1-2) Be imitators of God, Therefore, as dearly loved children (2) and live a life of love, just as Christ loved us as a fragrant offering and sacrifice to God.

Do not let anyone tell you how to run your show. If you fall from time to time, that is ok, get up and try it again. You will never learn unless you do it for yourself.

Imitating others can play out bad if these people are doing things that go against your spiritual beliefs. You should edify yourself in a way that shows your morals and integrity. However, you can be a leader and show others.

We have great leaders that have settled for being followers. That is sad; these people did not have enough faith in God or themselves to take the initiative to go boldly as leaders instead, they missed their mission by being in a following state of mind.

Therefore, my sisters go boldly and lead with your creativity, there are many people that regret not taken the initiative to lead their own lives, now they are living in regret. Do not let someone lead you into regret from you imitating him or her. Be yourself depending on God only. If you are going to imitate someone, let that someone be Jesus. When you start imitating others you begin to pick up spirits of the very thing you are imitating, which can cause you to become someone or something that is not of your character. Do not allow unwanted spirits in your life. Find out who you are and live your life with the spirit God has given you.

Never imitate other spirits, love who you are and work on being a better you. God wants us to be the image of Christ, God wants you to serve him with your creative gifts that he has blessed you with; you are not being fair to yourself or your father in Heaven when you take on the role of other attitudes. In order to have a fulfilled life you must start portraying your own character.

God made you an original human being, so you are to have you original talents. Your thoughts and talents should be your own. Create your business, home, family and ideas from your creative abilities; God loves us to showcase our talents especially when we glorify him.

WHAT IS ALL THE COMPETITION ABOUT?

Ladies, why are we in such competition with each other? I have always been disturbed about how competitive women are. Let me tell you something right now, "I am not in competition with anyone." I do not find that classy at all. I am a Diva and a child of the most high (GOD) I do not have to prove myself to anybody but, my father in Heaven.

Women have the tendency to drive themselves crazy to be better than the next woman. Stop the madness, if you would learn to love yourself

and start seeing yourself as God
sees you then competing with others
will become irrelevant. I see myself
as Jesus sees me as a precious gift; I
do not have to compete because I am
already special.

I would like every woman to be able
to recognize and understand it is not
about that negative energy that you
are wasting trying to outdo the next
person. You have to know who you
are as a woman and everything else
will fall into place. The next time you
feel you need to compete with
someone because, you think she has
something that you think is better.
Stop and think about how special

you are to God. Give yourself the love and attention that speaks,"Woman." Your spirit should be that of love not strife, competition stirs up spirits that takes you away from your character as a virtuous woman. You should have the confidence that God made you out of his image, which exemplifies the best.

Key Statement: Having a competitive spirit deprives you of your joy and success. (Proverbs 14:30) "A heart at peace gives life to the body but envy rots the bones."

STAY COMMITTED TO YOUR GOALS.

Stay committed to your goals that you are seeking; do not allow yourself to be distracted with trivial things. You should never rely on people to give you praise, it is ok to share with people, but your faith should be in the one who has the final say (GOD).

"Hallelujah I am Woman"

Do not fall prey to the naysayer. People will always find a reason to put you and your project down they will ridicule, spit venom, hate and try to crush your spirit, nevertheless, you keep doing what you are doing, regardless to what anybody has to say. You can do it and be successful with anything that you set your heart to do, but you must remain faithful to your cause. Stay prayerful and ask God for his strength to help you stay committed. You cannot lose with God; however, with man you can lose a lot why? Because usually you have to do something in return not only that, man will let you down And disappoint you for reasons so obvious, they do not want to see you do it.

I know this sound a bit negative, but I am a realist and tell it exactly how God has given it. When you are working on big projects stay focused on your plans. Stay committed to your goals; seek help from people that are already doing what you are trying to do and if that does not work, start your own resources by researching the field you would like to see become a reality. There is no room for failure.

"Hallelujah I am Woman"

You can make it and be successful at whatever you desire in life.

I remember my first project. People talked about me and what hurts is they are people I thought were my friends. I felt hurt because, I would have appreciated them talking to me instead of behind my back. God will always lead you to who is for you and away from who is not. He can give you peace concerning any situation.

When God lead you away from people believe me it is in your best interest to be obedient and walk away.

(Proverbs 13:20) "He who walks with the wise grows wise but companions of fools suffer harm."

God will never take anything away from you that he is not going to give better than what you lost. Regardless, to whatever or whoever it is, if you lose it trying to do the right thing God is going to give it back double for your trouble. God will not allow you to have negative burdens.

"Hallelujah I am Woman"

All you have to do is call on Jesus, he is right there with his loving spirit to guide you through your burdens. It is a blessing to know when we feel as if we cannot go on any longer, all we have to do is call on our Lord and savior Jesus Christ, he will take the burden and lighten the load. He never leaves us we leave him.

We need to get back to worship and praise, which in turn glorifies our father in Heaven, that we may know the power of God in our time of need. Whenever your burdens are heavy, you can call on Jesus to comfort you in your time of need.

Ladies, we have a safe haven in Jesus he will take care of you and bless you with the good of the land, but you must first seek God and give him the praise. I know many times we think, we need people to validate us, but, God is the only one we need to get approval for our destiny and success.

Key Statement: No matter what happens, continue towards your goals to success. *When you stay committed to your goals, you are demonstrating faith, and when we show God that we have faith no matter what, he will always bring you to victory and success.*

WATCH YOUR ASSOCIATES, ALWAYS PRAY

Always stay watchful in your environment. God wants us to stay safe in everything we do. Keep your eyes open, the devil will come as an angel of light, but have wolf tendencies to take you out!

(Luke 21:36) "Be always on the watch, and pray that you may be able to escape all that is about to happen, and that you may be able to stand before the Son of man."

Women are very susceptible to flattery. Some of us all a man have to do is tell us we are cute and bam! He is living in the house like a king on his throne. You do not know him from a can of paint but he is sleeping in your bed, every night. We have to be extra careful when we have children. There is so much happening to our children right in our homes, our children are not safe, and this is what happens when we allow the wrong people into our homes. Who is to say your newfound sweetie is someone you can trust to be around your children. Did you get any information on him? Always check out a potential date. It will not hurt to run a check on someone you want to get to know. I assure you there will be no regrets.

What you will regret is if you allow this person to come into your home and he molest your children and wreck complete havoc on everyone in the home. Never be anxious for anything including a man. Let God lead your man to you in his time. The bible says, **"Be anxious for nothing."**

I understand that it gets lonely sometimes; we all want to experience love and affection from the opposite sex. Being a woman entails a lot. Most of us are soul providers in our homes and that can be stressful at times. Therefore, you definitely do not need any added stress that may bring harm to you and your children.

I have found that when you wait on God, he is faithful he knows your needs, he hears your prayers, you are not alone God is just a prayer away. Keep yourself occupied with your dreams and work towards your goals. This will alleviate the tensions of loneliness. Stay on your mission to accomplish the things you set out to do, stay determined no matter what happens, Although, there will be obstacles. "I believe obstacles are there to keep us Motivated"

When you go through the storms, you will always come out stronger than you were before the storm. Victory will prevail; you have to stay the course to see the blessings. Storms in our lives are never comfortable, just remember they are only for a short time, joy will come.

Matthew (15:4) "When a blind man leads a blind man they both end up in the ditch."

Your blessings, healings, purpose and success comes when you are walking with the right people. There is a story about a frog and a scorpion. The scorpion needed help across the river because he could not swim. The frog says "but if I help you, you will sting me." "No way" the scorpion replied, "if I do we both will drown, now how about that ride?" The frog agreed and the Scorpion hopped on the frog's back, half way across the river the scorpion stings the frog. To the frog's surprise, he says, "Hey, you promised you wouldn't sting me." The scorpion shrugged and replied, "I'm a scorpion that's my nature." The moral of the story is the devil is a liar, bad relationships are like cancer and if not treated it will spread causing infection throughout the body. You must have the strength to walk away from toxic people and relationships that are no good for you. Surround yourself with positive people that care about you for who you are instead of what you have to offer. You cannot grow and have good health with deadness in your life. Although, some issues can be corrected with a person who have a willing heart that has developed a relationship with God. Sometimes, even then some people will not love or care for you, always see God in who should be in your life. You have to be careful what environments you encounter, there is always something or someone the devil will use to try to Destroy your Joy. If someone show you who he or she really is, believe him or her! We have choices in life; you have the ability to choose right from wrong.

When you are walking with God usually you will make the right decisions because you want to please your father (God).

The lord has kept me in my most trying times when the storms are raging, Jesus is there to restore and love you unconditionally. He will be everything to you, because he has a love for us that no one else can have for us. He has been my mother, father, brother, sister and best friend. I know what God is capable of doing. I have seen his holy hands *work in my life repeatedly. When he (the devil) thought, he had me God stepped in and brought me back to his gracious presence.*

There was a time when I was spinning out of control with destructive behaviors because of the hurt and pain I felt deep inside, what makes me so joyous is the fact that God protected me.

Key Statement: Always seek God's protection in your relationships with people. Watch and pray.

Remember to walk with people who have your best interest in mind. True friends will be there when you need them and you should reciprocate the same "Godly" love.

You never know when you are going to need that same person you have discarded. God has a way of bringing you back in that persons' path so be careful how you treat people, what goes around comes around. If you truly love Jesus and want his best, you need to start treating his people with the love he has commanded you to have. You never know when you are serving Jesus he can come in any form. Always honor your parents and see that they have their needs met. God has called you to be a blessing pray that God will bless you to be a blessing in someone who is less fortunate in life, this brings blessings back to you.

INNER PEACE

Your inner peace will require some changes to take place within you. There is nothing more unsettling than a person without peace. I am not talking about being in a peaceful atmosphere. I am talking about that peace that surpasses all understanding. The kind of peace that when someone does wrong to you, it is not effective; you just let it blow away with the wind. I have learned to focus my attentions on being a woman of grace.

I do not want anyone to think they have robbed me of anything. That control I will not allow. When someone angers you, you have given him or her control of you and your peace of mind.

(Isaiah 32:17) "The fruit of righteousness will be peace; the effect of righteousness will be quietness and confidence forever."

Control your emotions; women are emotional beings because of our ability to nurture. Nevertheless, too many times we allow our emotions to overrule our logic. We must walk in devotion; instead, the majority of us walk in emotions by falling in love too soon, with unrealistic dreams. Emotions can spin out of control causing you to drown in the sea of what you think is "love" you will never mature on emotions alone. When a relationship is over, it is over embrace Christ and learn to control your emotions. I have seen women lose it and seek vengeance by slashing tires, breaking windows, fighting and many other irrational actions. This is what happens when you cannot control your emotions. You set out to destroy the person who has rejected you; in reality, you make your self-look like a fool. The Lord says, **"Vengeance is his."** If *you have been mistreated and feel pain and despair, please do not cheapen your value as the woman you are. Let God handle it, you can not begin to discipline like God, so pray and let God take care of the battle, it's not yours anyway.*

Key Statement: Never allow your emotions to control you or allow anyone to control your emotions, Keep you inner peace.

Always be a virtuous woman in everything you do. When you can show your wisdom in a bad situation this shows maturity. Your peace is valuable and should never be subject to compromise. Peace is something you cannot buy, the peace that God gives you will bring you to a better understanding and a relationship with Jesus that is better than any pain Man, Woman or Child can cause. You do not have to bring your standards down to get your point across, keep your temperament in check, the enemy wants you to react by losing control of your tongue. The bible says **"a sweet answer turns away wrath".** *Therefore, choose to answer with grace even in the most trying times and watch how controlled God will allow the situation to turn around for your good. Do not letyour good works be evil spoken of.*

CLEAN YOUR SPIRITUAL HOUSE

Clean your spiritual house, in other words; in order to start your healing process, you may want to start by cleaning and renewing your spirit as if you are spring cleaning. Here are some things you can do to start this process.

• *Stop worrying about the small things that you have no control over.*

• *Throw out the past and all the pain and negative spirits that come along with it.*

• *Start some attainable goals short and long term.*

• *Speak positive life changing words into your spirit.*

Do not let the past things you have done haunt you any longer. It is not deserving of your time. Bring those positive things into your life by replacing those that are negative, rebuke useless spirits with God's loving spirit. You have to believe that God is going to see you through to victory and keep you safe from all harm. You have to keep the lines of communication open to your father in heaven. He wants us to speak to him daily, God wants you to have his best; he does not want us out here struggling with past hurts which often robs us of our joy time after time again. Your praise and being thankful to your father in heaven is what is going to bring your blessings into your life. Faith is the core of your trust in God.

God is pleased when we trust him with our lives. "Personally, there is no one on this earth I trust with my life." People have disappointed me excessively to trust anyone with my life. No one gets God's glory from me, but God. I remember an incident concerning my ex-husband and me; he was upset with me because he

thought I was supposed to put my faith in him. I let him know; that no *one will ever be an idol to me. God is the only one I bow down to for my life.*

Key Statement: Your faith should only be to God. Honor him with thanksgiving.

When we are thankful for what we have and are good stewards, God will give you more of his blessings. Having an ungrateful attitude will cause you to have less in life, so be thankful for your blessings so that you may have God's best.

"Hallelujah I am Woman"

Renewing your mind is the key to your spiritual connection to Christ. When you focus on things you have no control over this will cause you to have a cluttered spirit, clean that mess out of your life, start to focus on Jesus and look to him for your help he will lead you to a better life when you seek what pleases God.

"Hallelujah I am Woman"

Notes

HAVE A COURAGEOUS SPIRIT

Be courageous, (2 Timothy 1:7) says, "For God has not given you a spirit of fear; but of power, and of love and of a sound mind. Boldly walk, talk, and praise God.

You do not have to fear anyone but God and that is a loving fear to do the right thing. You have power over your enemies, so why do you allow them to keep tormenting you? Women, we have strength and courage that lies within us that defines true **"WOMAN"** when you believe in your heart and know in your spirit that God is your true source, you will be able to courageously, reach many goals.

All of your hopes and dreams will be attainable; however, you must believe and have a spirit of courage. A strong courageous woman shows confidence in the midst of her storms; she shows the world she is a woman of strength, courage, faith, hope and all good things of the lord. Doors will open, bodies will be healed, and victory will be yours in the mighty name of Jesus. Stand strong on the word, weakness is of the enemy.

God gave us authority over all things, start speaking the word of God boldly to your circumstances, command those things to line up with the word, you have the ability to have every blessing God has for you. Jesus says you have not because you ask not. When you pray believe it and claim it in the name of Jesus.

If it be God's will you will have just what you ask. Humble yourself to the anointing of the Holy Spirit, ask God to turn your situation around that you can walk in his blessings courageously speaking his will.

YOUR HAPPINESS AS A WOMAN

Give up the need to be "perfect" no one is perfect. Start to bring balance into your life by being optimistic. Everyday do something positive that will influence others.

"Dream big, realize your power as a woman, if you can conceive the thoughts in your mind and believe it in your heart, you are able to achieve it in your life."

Learn to balance your life with self-care and fulfillment, by nurturing your heart, mind, and spirit. Keep your mind ready for success.

Be a good friend, the kind of friend you want in your life. When we treat people with respect and concern, it will in turn come back to you. True love for friends and family will heighten your spirits and your blessings from God will Be many. When you have true happiness in your life it is hard for people to miss because, everyone you come in contact with will feel your warmth, when we are happy we are sympathetic to others and their needs. Happy people, have happy lives because they are cheerful givers. God loves a cheerful giver. Stop! Being selfish, that is not a spirit that God likes, he cannot bless you when you are selfish to others. God wants us to take care of one another.

When you see another sister struggling and working hard to keep food on the table and a roof over her children's head and you have the means to help her but you selfishly do not, then my sister or brother, I feel sorry for you and pray God's mercy on you because you just slapped God in his face. Do not ever

let being selfish cause you to miss
true happiness.

**Key Statement: When you have
true happiness you treat others
with love and empathy.**

**Proverbs 19:17 he who is kind to
the poor lends to the lord and he
will reward him.**

God is pleased with us when we look
out for one another. Selfishness
takes away from your spiritual
being, which in turn can cause you to
become spiritually wicked. Love your
neighbor as you would love your self.
I am not saying you

have to be all in their business and visiting everyday. However, treat everyone with the respect that you would like to have, notice; God is watching us.

Notes

WALK IN VICTORY

Romans (8:28) says "And we know that all things work together for good to them that love God, who is called according to his purpose.

Women, we have a purpose in life, we are more than conquerors. We should walk in victory at all times knowing that you have the victory over every situation, every circumstance tells our father that you are working the purpose of your being. We, have the victory as women, we are the strength that carries life.

For too long now we have been treated as the lesser one, the one of no value, the one that is of no consequence. However, women I am here to tell you that God has given us the victory, power and a sound foundation to go boldly and declare the things that are our inheritance. God gave man specific orders to respect his wife, to love, honor, and cherish her and treat her as he would himself. For no man mistreats himself do he? Do you know your husband is supposed to be willing to die for you? Man is given specific Instructions, because woman is only supposed to back man up, not do his job. According to Journal Magazine, single women head more than 45% of households in the United States. This is not the order God had planned.

Men have overstepped their boundaries with God, by leaving their positions as the head of the family. I tell you this day all UN Godly Men will have to repent before God for the ways they have treated their families. God is not sleep he will give his daughters the victory over all our enemies. He will prepare our tables before them and make them our footstools. God is going to have *his glory he speaks about these things that is now taking place.*

(2 Timothy 3, 1-6) but mark this there will be terrible times in the last days. People will be lovers of themselves, lovers of money, boastful, proud, abusive, and disobedient to parents, ungrateful, unholy. Without love, unforgiving, slanderous, brutal, not lovers of the good, treacherous, rash, conceited, lovers of pleasure rather than lovers of God. Have nothing to do with them. (6) They are the kind that worm their way into the homes of weak-willed women who

are loaded down with sins and are swayed by all kinds of evil desires always learning but never able to acknowledge the truth.

This is the very reason we need to trust God at all times, especially when we are seeking a companion, you do not want that misery in your home. God has his men and they are the warriors out here establishing their Godly worth. Therefore, women claim your peace, strength, faith and courage shout all victory! When you look at the news and see another child or woman that have been killed at the hands of these demonic spirits think twice about whom you are associating yourself. You are the high priced virtuous woman with a worth that surpasses all that mess.

When you can sleep peaceful at night, shout victory! When you can come and go as you please shout victory! Stand righteous before God, live out your purpose as the woman that God has called you to be. What the enemy meant for bad, God will turn it around in your favor. Put the devil under your feet and exemplify your authority, my sister, walk in victory. Our God is a God of victory. I do not know a man that can defeat him.

God has given us victory to walk in favor as we speak the will of God. When troubles creep up, speak victory knowing by faith you have the victory, will set God and the holy angels in place to fight all your enemies.

THANK GOD WITH YOUR PRAYER.

We must remember to thank God always in our prayers. **Proverbs speaks of the virtuous woman. She is up early thanking God in prayer and praise.**

Proverbs (31:10) "Who can find a virtuous woman? For her price is far above rubies.

We should be thankful for what God is in our lives, "he is our lives." When you give God honor in your praise, he brings forth favor and blessings that are not of your power. Do not allow yourselves to be fooled, none of what you do is you, it is all God. I hear people say how they have made it on their own giving themselves glory for their accomplishments. God should get all the honor and praise for every goal and all success that you have encountered. Many women are at a place where all hope is gone. They cannot seem to get pass the same rut that keeps them down year after year. Many are stuck in a life of hell only speaking negative towards their future and despising anyone that has a better life than theirs or so they think, speak life: We must learn to speak blessings and miracles of God into our households. Glorify God;

give him the praise for your life. You will have the things that you speak; thanking God will cause the desires of your heart to come into your life.

I know it can be hard sometimes. No matter what, you can make it through, keep the faith. Surrender all and allow God to come into your life and heal your pain and despair, he loves us, when we are thankful to him for being our father he draws closer to us and gives us comfort no one is capable of giving. God will take you from misery to joy; he loves you and wants you to have a fulfilled life.

"Hallelujah I am Woman"

Everything we do should glorify our father in heaven. The more praises go up, the more blessings come down. Praise God, for your joy, praise God even in your storms this will bring you closer to God so when he hear your righteous cries he will answer and deliver you out of all your distress.

HAVE CONFIDENCE THAT GOD IS IN CONTROL

Have confidence that God knows your needs and your hearts desires. God has not forgotten you. He will bring all things forth in his time; God's time is not our time.

We may want something to happen right now however, God knows exactly when it should happen that is why he says, **"be anxious for nothing"** *Ecclesiastes 3: 1 states:* **"There is a time for everything and a season for every activity under heaven."**

"Hallelujah I am Woman"

God has a plan if we stay focused on doing what we need to do to bring peace and well-being into our lives. I thank God for creating the woman that I am now. I know that I can always depend on God when I cannot depend on anyone else. I know I can call on the mighty name of Jesus and he will cause my help to come.

I know my worth as a woman and I am a good woman. The man that God blesses to have me is going to be a very blessed man.

Ultimately, everything that I do to this God filled man will be to honor God.

"Hallelujah I am Woman"

Today, I have just what God showed me he would do in my life. That inner peace I spoke of earlier is mine. I will not let anyone take that from me. If you allow people to take your peace, everything about you will fall under an unrewarding life. We are in a time that love is not a priority for the most anymore. It is all about self. I have encountered some very selfish spirits in people in the last five years that I have never seen before. I have true love that abounds from my father in heaven.

"Hallelujah I am Woman"

This love that I have brings peace in my spirit; this is why no one can have it. I will always have that spirit that will set off spirituality, because you cannot buy what God has given me. My sister, it is my honor that you are reading this book at this time. God knows just what you need before you need it. He will never let you down. When, I think about the goodness of God my soul cries, "Hallelujah! I am woman."

You are a prized gift given of God. That is something to be thankful for; the time has come for women everywhere to start righteously claiming their positions.

"Hallelujah I am Woman"

Yes, I know you have been beaten, raped, abused and tossed aside.

However, it's time to let it go! And throw those wicked evil Spirits back in the pit of hell where they belong and take up your crowns and assume your positions.

You are valuable and worthy of the love you seek that will edify you as the virtuous woman you are. Strive for excellence to prevail in your life, always seek the positive. Let negative things be of the past, push forward to your goals and make your

dreams realities that everyone can see that you are a woman that is mighty and powerful in Jesus. Show your strength, weakness is of the enemy. It is time to stop being the victim and be the victor.

Key Statement: Be courageous in everything you do. Boldly go about doing the will of God.

Seek God boldly, when you pray ask God boldly for what you need of him although, he already knows our needs we must yet, come to the throne with boldness; also speak God's will boldly to others. That confidence is what God is looking for in his children when you know that God has the control over all things you can walk in confidence, leading others to Christ. Your salvation depends on how confident you are in the work of the Holy Spirit. Your confidence in God will allow everyone you encounter to see the power of God in your life, this is that drawing power that will bring all miracles of God into your life, and this is when you are going to be able to bless many.

LEAVE THOSE BAD BOYS ALONE.

Bad boys are just that bad! Sure, they seem exciting, that is their game. They want to be exciting to every woman they encounter. When they are finished with you, they move on to another, you are not the flavor anymore.

A bad boy has no conscience of how to treat a woman; their mentality is not mature enough to handle a virtuous woman. Most bad boys are immature, life is only a party to them they do not know real commitment. You worth exceeds anything he can imagine because he has no value of who he really is so therefore, he cannot commit anything real or lasting with you as a woman.

When I was young, I liked bad boys too, but soon found out that I was unhappy living the fast life they offer. **I am a "Godly woman" who loves "Godly men," "if he can't pray, he certainly can't lay."**

Ladies, if you have the bad boy syndrome, I know you are living a lie. The bad boy cannot offer you true happiness. That happiness you seek can only come from God who has your best interest at heart. Remember, your man is supposed to be willing to die for you. Ask your bad boy if he is willing to do that. I can tell you; (No) he is often too selfish to take care of you when you are sick, how is he going to die for you? He does not know your worth and if you are with him, neither do you. A woman that knows her worth would not give the bad boy the time of day.

(2 Corinthians 6:14) "Do not be yoked together with unbelievers. For what do righteousness and wickedness have in common? Or what fellowship can light have with darkness?

A woman that knows she is a gift of God will not allow disrespect of any kind. Do not allow you to be taken for granted or mistreated in any way. I was talking to a young woman that thought if her man did not beat her, he did not love her. This is a beautiful gifted woman who was being lead straight to the pit of hell with lies. I counseled this woman extensively about her worth as a woman, and now today, she is making a change in her life. Your situation can change but you have to take the initiative to bring about the needed change you want to see happen.

"Hallelujah I am Woman"

I encountered another young woman as well. She confessed to me that when she was young, two of her family members had molested her. She poured her heart out to me about how she felt she was not worthy of being loved because she was promiscuous; She felt nasty and hated herself. Her family and everyone around her called her filthy names such as whore, slut, tramp and more vile undeserving names that she had been associating her worth with for all these years. I listened to her as she cried with a pain in her heart that brought tears to my eyes.

"How dare a mother allow someone to molest her child, and then make her suffer for the abuse?" I reassured this young woman that was not her fault the guilt she was carrying was from the pit of hell and she had every right to live a life without shame and disgust. We talked for many hours. I found this young woman to be quite intelligent and very articulate as well. No one has ever bothered to hear her dreams. They were too negative and destroying to realize that a great woman was sitting in their presence .We cannot let our

past lives define who we are. You see if we let our past, have our future then we have done ourselves an injustice. No one is going to tie me to my past, those things are old news, the woman I am today is what counts.

A lot of us were probably just as promiscuous as that young woman, or did some other ungodly things, because one thing for sure we all have a past. Let it go, grow up, do not let anyone call you nasty things that are in the past life you once lived. This is why Jesus came that we may have life and have it more abundant.

Jesus already paid the price for your sins why should you keep paying for them repeatedly. There is no reason for it. Lift your heads up and move on with your life.

God is good and faithful to bring you to a blessed state of mind. Always remember you are a beautiful being that God created for greatness. Your purpose is to uplift and bring life to you and others. Your destination should always end in excellence. Because you see, that was then, this is now. The Devil knows your worth that is why he preys on women with low self-esteem.

He sends you the **"Bad Boy"** *they know they can get away with mistreating you because your concept of yourself is low and they love to approach a woman with that mentality because she is easy to treat just as he wants to treat her. He knows he will not get much of a fight for respect. Remember my sister, God loves you in spite of your past you can make a change in your life and live it with joy, love, abundance and blessings. Allow God to come into your life right now, he can heal and restore your soul. Let go, give it to the master of your* *destiny. Speak with boldness that you are a woman! A woman, of virtue and excellence! "Hallelujah I am Woman"!*

(Ephesians 6:10-11) "Finally, be strong in the lord and in his mighty power. (11) Put on the whole armor of God so that you can take your stand against the devil's schemes."

Do not fool yourself into thinking you can dance with the devil. You cannot date bad boys and live a life of holiness the two do not mix, one spirit will overrule the other and if you do not have the strength to deal with the street life you will fall considerably. God is faithful and just, he will keep you on the right course when you are seeking the Kingdom. The bad boy only knows the Kingdom of the streets.

KEEP YOURSELF ADORNED FOR GREATNESS

Ladies, please, keep yourself up that you do not fall into depression. I know at times it can get stressful with all the responsibilities of working and running a household, but you should maintain your appearance. Stay abreast of your outer appearance. I am not saying that you need to run out and spend a fortune; however, you should make sure that you are neat in appearances when going out into the public eye. Men are visual they find us women attractive when we take care of ourselves. If you are looking to have a man approach you then you should be approachable by looking your best at least neat that he may find you attractive enough to hold a conversation with. If money is tight you can find trendy outfits that will accommodate your budget, match things together, add a little make up, a nice hairstyle, and there you have it. Keeping yourself looking refreshed tells everyone around you that you care about yourself. Although, your true beauty comes from with in, that inner beauty that exerts itself to shine for everyone to see. Smile, It cost nothing to speak to everyone you encounter you never know who you are speaking to. "A bad attitude is like a car with four flat tires it will get you nowhere." Teach your children how to respect, and value life, it will pay in ways you cannot imagine. Celebrate your beauty; this builds confidence, your self-esteem will lift as you groom for success, this will Strengthen your spirit to conquer all that you encounter.

Key Statement: Ladies when we look our best we feel good and can accomplish our dreams.

WHO DEFINES YOUR BEAUTY?

The world defines beauty as a size six bikini. God defines it in your spirit. This is what makes us unique the different shapes, colors, personalities and so forth. We are not all meant to be a size six; women are dying to be thin, why? Because society says if you are not a size six you are not beautiful. "Jesus rebukes, and bounds that demon that has robbed us sisters of our self-

image. I plead the blood of Jesus in your spirit that you are beautiful and acceptable to God."

No, we should not abuse ourselves by over eating that is a sin within itself, but to be a full figured woman is not a sin you are still God's child and he loves you as you are. If a man leaves you for gaining weight after years of marriage, giving birth to his children and being the faithful woman that you are, then my sister let him go, he is not the person God meant to be in your life in the first place. Anytime someone has conditions that would limit their love for me, scares me.

"Hallelujah I am Woman"

When you start putting conditions on love, you have taken real love and made a joke of it. Jesus has no conditions to the love he has for you. He can love you right where you are he died for you. Now, that is real love. God gave his only begotten son that you may have life and have it more abundant. The nerve of someone to walk into your life and make you feel unloved when our father in heaven gave you as a gift to man! That is the true definition of your beauty. Can I get a **"Hallelujah?"** *Women, we are so beautiful never mind what they call you; you will never be any of those* *ungodly expressions, your beauty is in your heart and spirit. Whatever you exemplify from your heart is where your beauty lies, I hope that as a woman your beauty exemplify, the grace of God almighty, and the love he has for you as the woman he has called you to be.*

Key Statement: Beauty is only skin deep, your true beauty lies in your spirit. *When a man is interested in a woman, he sees beyond your physical attributes, he is more interested in knowing who you are as a woman. Show your beauty from the inside out. Let your* *light shine that God gets the glory, only then, are you truly beautiful.*

KEEP YOUR TEMPLE HOLY UNTO

THE LORD.

You take him back when he has taken you for granted, then, regret that you let him come back. Because, of your fear of being alone. The man that is supposed to love and cherish you constantly plays you. Fornicating, committing adultery against God because you think he loves you, but in all truthfulness, you are just his booty call or flavor for the month, or week. You hold out for a while thinking if you demand his respect he will realize what he has but sister, quit fooling yourself he never cared in the first place he just wanted what you had to offer in the flesh to quench his sexual desires, leaving you empty and sin laden, he got what he wanted; now when you call he messes with your mind. Making you feel less than the woman you are. You have feelings for a brother that devalues your worth and leave you empty and unfulfilled.

Sister, that man can not fulfill you or your deepest desires, needs, spirituality or your cries for real love, some things you can only get from Jesus. Sex is never the answer, it is a temporary relief that can cause a multitude of pain and disappointment, don't expect different results, while you're still acting the same, change your ways by exerting your worth, the only way he is going to see your worth is when you show respect to yourself, love who you are and keep your temple undefiled by the tricks of the enemy. He (The Devil) knows your worth that is why he is targeting to destroy you as a woman. God has called you to be a blessing. You are to stay alert, do not give in to the tricks of the enemy and if you do, do not beat yourself up for it, repent and ask God to forgive you. Do not keep blaming yourself when he is to blame, (The Devil). We all make mistakes it is human to fall short. Nevertheless, I know you are hurt, be patient your king will come because not all brothers are the same; some are still immature they have not recognized the woman's worth. I know the times we live in are not easy from day to day but please, escape from the trends. Stop playing the harlot, although, you say they're just your "friends" Make him cherish the inner person that is within you, make him work for your heart before you consider sharing your most precious jewels, giving away your valuable goods for recreation, this is spiritual desecration, which can lead you straight to hell, in return you feel cheap and worthless. There is nothing wrong in waiting for the right man to come into your heart and give you the love you deserve as a woman. In addition, any brother who knows your worth will certainly have the patience to wait on your gifts.

A woman who knows her worth is a Woman so awesome and powerful, a Woman worthy of a man that is a righteous man after God's own heart. Stop dating busters you have seen their messed up lives. They cannot offer you real love or anything else for that matter................

"Hallelujah I am Woman"

If he is not responsible, or support your dreams, why waste your time? With someone who cannot see your value as the gift God has given to him as a blessing to benefit his life. With man content with being a "baby's daddy" and you being a "baby's mama" is out of God's plan for the family structure that he created. Does he tell you he loves you? Better yet, does he show you that you are valuable to him? A real man will do all he has to, to make sure that you know he is a man that sees you as his valuable woman given by his father in heaven. The Bible instructs wives to submit, however, only to a man that is worthy of your love, to a man who will not dodge child support to buy useless items, hundred dollar sneakers, and self fulfilling parties with women who don't have any morals or respect. Don't fall in love with UN Godly men; instead walk in Grace, life is like a tornado tearing apart those trying to make it on pure emotion. Draw close to Christ and then if a brother ever questions your worth you can boldly let him know that you are a virtuous woman who is waiting on the lord. **(1 Corinthians 6:18-20) "Flee from sexual immortality. All other sins a man commits are outside his body. (19) Do you not know that**

your body is the temple of the Holy Spirit, who is in you, whom you received from God? You are not your own. (20) You were bought at a price, therefore honor God with your body.

Ladies, do not sleep with a man just because he wants you to, let him know how you feel if you are waiting for your wedding day, tell him, then stand strong on God's word. I know these days and times waiting until you are married is almost unheard of but, that's what sets you apart from the rest and make you so unique in God's eyes and the man that is pursuing you. He will have more respect for you because of who you are and God will bless you tremendously for being a faithful servant.

Key Statement: Love is not sex, a man who has true love for you will respect your body.

YOU CAN OVERCOME THE STORMS.

The storms we face in life can be challenging for the most part. Pain and suffering is never comfortable. Most discomforts we have been through in our lives have taken us to a higher level in strength. I know for most of us we have been through some storms that have caused us to feel total brokenness. Unbelievably, those storms build the strength we need to triumph. There are many of us going through some storms in our lives as I write this book; my encouragement to you is to stay prayerful, keep your faith in God, do not give up continue to stand steadfast. The battle is almost over and if you stand strong, you will triumph to victory. God wants us to acknowledge him in everything we do. He is everything to us without God we are nothing. My storms have been many, I have seen battles that only God could fight for me, and I have learned that the battle is not ours, it belongs to the Lord and when we let him fight our battles, we always come out the winner. When we try to fight these demonic forces, we can get overwhelmed; the fact of the matter is we are not fighting with flesh and blood we are fighting with principalities of darkness in high places. Therefore, we need to leave the battles to God who can go in, take our victory, and hand it to us on a platinum platter. The storms that I have been through has been the kind of things that would make most people want to cut their wrist, what kept me going was the fact that I knew God was in the midst and he was carrying me at that time, because my strength was not strong enough to do the battle.

There have been times when God has shown up himself on my behalf. That is one of my many reasons I can shout "Hallelujah, I am woman." With boldness that comes from deep within my spirit. I can shout all glory to the king! He is my king, lord, and savior; I praise him with no regrets or shame. Sisters, if you want to overcome your storms and move to a blessed life let Jesus in your life, move out of the way, and let God.

I assure you that in the midst of your storm you will gain strength of many men and a spiritual renewing. When it is all said and done you will shine like new money, you see a diamond sits under pressure; the more pressure the brighter the diamond. Remember the worth of rubies. That is you girl, a Ruby has to go through fire, the hotter the flames the more beautiful the Ruby. Forget about what someone has done or is doing, leave it to God and your battle is already won.

God knows what it is going to take to overcome your circumstances. You will never be able to handle it like God. Women we must keep ourselves under the blood of Jesus as we take on our challenges and as we start on our journeys, we must first seek the protection of the Holy Spirit to accommodate us as we seek our goals to become successful.

"Hallelujah I am Woman"

Notes

Do not give up!

When it hurts call on God, take a deep breath, and let it out. I know you are hurting and confused, and you just do not know what to do. You are walking around wondering why your life is in turmoil. You are trying to figure out why you have to go through all of this hurt and pain. The betrayals, lies, beatings, mind games, and disrespect.

I know you trusted him to be there through the good and the bad. When all hell broke out, he was the last person to show you that he cared. This is why God said to put your trust in Him, not man. The storm will not last forever. Trust in Jesus. I have been there before. All you have to do is call on God and ask him to help you through it. He loves you, and unlike people, He will never leave or forsake you.

You do not have to be ashamed of your mistakes. God forgives and forgets.

Stop allowing the enemy to come into your mind and tell you the bad things you have done, and how no one cares if you are dead or alive. The devil is a liar! God has a purpose and a plan for your life. You have to surrender your all to God, and ask him to be the head of your life. Tell

"Hallelujah I am Woman"

God you need Him to lead and guide you. Ask him to remove anyone and anything that comes to hinder your walk with him, and to give you the strength to endure whatever may come your way. Don't you dare give up!

You have a purpose in life! My sisters enough is enough let your worth expedite through your works as the virtuous woman you are. Your destiny is for excellence and the successes you have in the mighty name of Jesus you are a woman of Strength. You are the pillar of life in Jesus, you can accomplish every task given by our father in Heaven you are beautiful and cherished by God. The blood of Jesus anoints you. **You are WOMAN! Shout Hallelujah,** because you have made it through the storm. You have accepted Jesus as your savior. Hold on to your faith no matter what happens, if your husband leaves you. The children act out, you lose you car, house, job regardless or whatever it may be continue to press forward with your goals and dreams of being successful and watch how God will move on your behalf. I hope that I have been a blessing to help you as a woman to see your *worth. We are conquerors, laborers in Jesus, never; let anyone take your joy.*

When you let someone take your joy, you will fall into depression. This is what the enemy wants, he wants you to doubt God and steal your faith because he knows once he gets your faith there is not too much else he can take away because your faith in God is what is going to keep you seeking after righteousness. Of course, the devil does not want you to have a fruitful life he wants your life destroyed.

Notes

AN UNFORGIVING HEART WILL

KILL YOUR SPIRIT

Maintain a forgiving spirit so that you will have balance, first you must forgive yourself and then others.

Forgiveness is for your spiritual healing. Let it go and let God. You cannot do anything with it except make yourself ill. God cannot work with an unforgiving spirit. You have to forgive, no matter what, you have to forgive and let God lift you up. You will not have any peace until you learn to let it go. Your health both physical and spiritual depends on you letting go of those negative spirits that cause you more harm than good.

Why would you allow yourself to stress over someone else's negative actions against you? You are up late nights worrying about that mess and they are in their beds sleeping sound as a rock. Let it go! God can work that out to your best. Yes, I know it hurts when someone do dirt to you. I was married for many years to find out my husband was being unfaithful to me and what make it so bad is it was with a relative; my children and I suffered that sin along with him as long as I was holding a grudge, I could not move forward. My children and I were in a destitute state because of his actions.

I hated him for what he did to our children and me, I had many sleepless nights, did things that were out of my character trying to get revenge that only hurt me and my children. Nevertheless, the Holy Spirit stepped in and I had to give it up!

In addition, when I did God started to move in ways I did not understand. So, let it go, you have the victory over hurt, depression, and *a broken heart. God will work it out. I am a living witness to the miracles of God concerning healing from a broken heart. Do not allow yourself to cry another day, continue praying, walking, and talking with your father in heaven.*

Do not worry anymore about what is happening with the person who hurt you, you may see it as if they are living it Up. Maybe so, but, I know God will have the last say about what the end result will be. Stay faithful in your prayers and watch the blessings flow. Here are some things you can do to bring peace from some of the stresses that being unforgiving can cause.

TRY THESE STRESS RELIEVERS

• *Take a class to educate yourself.*

• *Meditate on the things of God.*

• *Light some candles and take a warm bubble bath, relax and let your mind flow.*

• *Try something you have never done before for instance: a book club, craft, volunteer for a cause you are interested in.*

• *Start a business with something you enjoy doing.*

There are many things you can do with your time. Do not sit around allowing your soul to die from being unforgiving. Take your life back, stop dwelling on the things of the past. When it is over, it is over. Take care of yourself that you live!

As long as you hold on to those unforgiving spirits, you are literally killing yourself. Do something constructive with your life to bring your spirit back into balance. God is pleased when we are forgiving one to another. Jesus says, "We must forgive one another in order for him to forgive us before his father in heaven."

DISPLAY CHARACTER

GOD *allows trials to build our character. There are so many women that have gone through different trials depression, divorce, abusive relationships, loneliness, abortion, rape, and much more. I am here to tell you that God is able to deliver you from any and everything that has a stronghold on your mind and heart. God is bigger than the trials. During the trials, we can become bitter, bitterness blocks your blessings, joy, love, and happiness.*

Sisters, there is no time for us to be bitter. The gap between life and death is so important.

Ephesians,(4:31 -32) "put away from you all bitterness and wrath and anger and wrangling and slander, together with all malice,

And be kind to one another, tenderhearted, forgiving one another, as God has forgiven you."

Let go of the hurt and pain, let God have his way. Pray and ask God for the strength to forgive, trust God he has never failed you yet. Take charge and seek your purpose in life.

God bless you and Heaven smile on you. Character is the virtue of a Godly Woman.

Key Statement: Take charge of your lives by faith and allow God to lead you through to success.

I am woman strong yet, sensitive. I am woman with creativity, which holds my mystery. I am woman made from man, to help him to enhance the land. I am woman; anointed, nurturing and loving I am woman my worth is set higher than hills. My virtue can never be compromised with deals.

"Hallelujah I am Woman"!

Conclusion

I am so pleased that I am able to share with you God's word for us as women and the worth that God has given us. I hope that this book has been an encouragement to you to start seeking the worth that you are entitled as a Daughter of the highest King.

Thank you for allowing me to illuminate some of the issues that plague us as women. I hope that I have caused you to think about the love that God has for us. God wants us to have his best and when we do not live according to his best we are depreciating his word and our value as one of the greatest gifts God has created. Be blessed in all that you do and think, always having a spirit of joy to edify your soul that you may see the true Blessings of God know your purpose; bring your dreams to realities as you hold on to Jesus. Stay the spiritual Diva that you are and in due season you shall reap what God has promised.

(Proverbs 22:1) "A good name is more desirable than great riches; to be esteemed is better than silver and gold."

In remembrance of my Mother Leola Knight Jacobs. A true woman of virtue. Thank you Mother for teaching me to love myself and being a leader in my life. I love you

January 7, 1932- March 3, 2012

"Hallelujah I am Woman"

www.ingramcontent.com/pod-product-compliance
Lightning Source LLC
Chambersburg PA
CBHW051959090426
42741CB00008B/1462